# PRAISE FOR *TRIUMPH!*

"So many guys in the NFL don't realize the great opportunity that they have until it's gone. The reality is that the NFL stands for Not For Long and they need to maximize every opportunity to give them a game plan for the rest of their life. *Triumph!* teaches all athletes exactly what it means to be grounded. It should serve as a blueprint for anyone who wants to play at the highest level on and off the field."

—**Renaldo Wynn,** Notre Dame Team Captain, NFL 1st Round Draft Pick as Defensive End, Jacksonville Jaguars (NFL All Rookie Team), Washington Redskins (Team Captain), New Orleans Saints, New York Giants. Currently a motivational speaker and working at Joe Gibbs Racing in business development under mentor Hall of Fame Coach Joe Gibbs as well as an ESPN and ACC college football analyst.

"An excellent book! It will definitely change lives, and it may just change sports as we know it!"

—**Mike McCoy,** Notre Dame Football All-American, NFL 1st Round Draft Pick, Green Bay Packers, Oakland Raiders, New York Giants, Detroit Lions, President of Mike McCoy Ministries

"Having coached at the collegiate level, I can tell you that the principles inside *Triumph!* are priceless. Not only will this book give players a process to compete at the highest levels, but more importantly it will help prepare them for all of life's future challenges."

—**Coach John Shingler,** former Notre Dame football player and football coach at Middle Tennessee State, Georgia Southern, University of Georgia, and Urbana College

"Good teams all do the same things to prepare, yet the intangibles are what determine whether they become great. *Triumph!* addresses all those intangibles and will truly prepare you to be a champion both on and off the field!"

—**Coach Tim McFarlin**, 34-year Georgia High School football coach at Roswell HS and Blessed Trinity HS, 2006 State Champion


"The lessons I learned from Coach Matt on the football field I carry to this day with me in my everyday life. For example, if the ball doesn't bounce your way, that's when you find out what you're made of. Not everything in life will be in your favor, but how you handle yourself in the face of adversity is all that matters. As you read through *Triumph!,* soak it all in. It will make you a champion in more ways than one."

—**Ali Rezvan**, University of Georgia student, economics major, former President of Alpharetta HS Future Business Leaders of America


"A must-read toolkit for any young athlete. With the game being 90% mental, *Triumph!* gives you 100% to win."

—**Aaron Hall**, former inside linebacker, Purdue University


"Anyone involved in sports should have a copy of this book and read it between each season. It will remind them why the game is played, and they will come away with a fuller appreciation of what it means to live in and be a part of God's creation."

—**Jeff Auterson**, President of Auterson Baseball


"I loved *Triumph!* A great read for leaders on and off the field!"

—**Adam Orkin**, youth baseball coach, CEO Orkin & Associates, Chairman of the Orkin Family Foundation

"This book should be in the libraries of all players, parents, and coaches. Matt's unique experience and background, along with his strong Christian faith, will give you a perspective that is truly uplifting."

—**Chuck Pendleton**, former athlete and youth football coach

# TRIUMPH!

## An Athlete's Guide to Winning On and Off the Field

Matt Kunz

Booktrope Editions
Seattle WA 2015

Cover Design by Greg Simanson
Proofreading by Christina Correnti

Hardcover ISBN: 978-1-62015-851-7
Print ISBN 978-1-62015-692-6
EPUB ISBN 978-1-62015-703-9

Library of Congress Control Number: 2015935131

*To my parents.*

*Mom, thanks for instilling in me the importance of faith.*

*Dad, you'll always be a Hall of Famer in my book.*

# TABLE OF CONTENTS

# FOREWORD BY
# COACH LOU HOLTZ

I have said many times to my players that nothing is ever as great as it seems, and nothing is ever as bad as it seems. Immediately after we won the National Championship in 1988, I called my team around me and told them that that moment was not the most important moment in their lives. No, what was more important was that the players had understood the character necessary to win for their future wives, families, and businesses.

You see, attitude drives winning. Everybody in the world will tell you why you can't, but it takes a strong belief in yourself to remind you why you can. All too often players become convinced that they can't when the opportunity to win is deep inside. Fortunately, a good coach can help bring out that winning attitude in his players.

Having read *Triumph! An Athlete's Guide to Winning On and Off the Field,* I was quite impressed at the can-do attitude presented for the everyday athlete. This book presents the right perspective to create a winning game plan for every athlete, regardless of age or sport. It definitely prepares the athlete not only for the challenges he'll face in sports, but also those challenges he'll face in life. I wish it had been available to me before I got into coaching, as it might have helped me better relate to the perspective of the athlete.

I'm proud to recommend that you read *Triumph!* Reread it before every season. And then, may you face your challenges courageously with a smile on your face and a song in your heart!

Coach Lou Holtz
*Notre Dame Head Football Coach (1986–1996)*
*1x National Champion (1988)*
*Founder of the Lou's Lads Foundation*

# FOREWORD BY
# COACH ARA PARSEGHIAN

In the era of social media and 24-hour news, it seems the pressures on today's athletes have been magnified to extreme levels. Coaches today are making far more than they did a generation ago. High school stadiums are looking more and more like college campuses. Commercialization has entered our arenas with large screen jumbotrons. Worse, it appears social media is hyping the me-first mentality among our young athletes. How many times do we read about a prominent athlete who finds himself in trouble? Even worse, how many athletes do we *not* read about because they drop out of sports due to the pressure created by misguided coaching or organizational politics? It seems the whole industry is missing the point.

Even in the days when I was the head football coach at the University of Notre Dame, many of the same pressures existed. Human nature then was the same as it is now. Fortunately, by adhering to certain principles and remembering our faith, we were able to teach our athletes that winning was the result of a process which, if followed, would help them learn to face their lives with confidence once their athletic careers ended. It must have worked because not only did we win two National Championships, but more importantly we sent our athletes out into the world to become good husbands, fathers, and leaders in their businesses and their communities.

After reading *Triumph! An Athlete's Guide to Winning On and Off the Field*, I couldn't help but think how timely this book is. *Triumph!* is a guide for every athlete, parent, or coach at any level of sports to read before every season. It helps athletes understand clearly how to approach their sport philosophically and practically. It also helps them understand the politics of sports, why certain things may be happening, and what they can do about it. Finally, it reminds athletes that they won't achieve success on their own, that success is helped by those around them, and especially that our faith plays a vital role.

The wisdom and principles in *Triumph!* transcend today's fast-paced world. In fact, this book simplifies sports by reminding us what's important and why we play the game in the first place. I'm confident that reading *Triumph!* will not only help give you a competitive edge, but it will do what it says and make you a winner both on and off the field.

Coach Ara Parseghian
*Notre Dame Head Football Coach (1964–1974)*
*2x National Champion (1966, 1973)*
*Founder of the Ara Parseghian Medical Research Foundation*

# INTRODUCTION

There was the picture of me in the Show Low paper. All of eight years old, I was running with all my might after rounding third. I could make it. Never mind that my coach was waving me to stop; I was going to score! What was he thinking, telling me to slow down? I could beat the throw to third base. Besides, that third baseman didn't have anything on me!

Yet there it was in black and white in the small town sports section for everyone to see: the third baseman from the opposing team with his glove holding the ball, and his glove touching the numbers on the back of my jersey. I had rounded third to get to home plate. A few steps later I was out and everyone in town saw it. When the local paper showed up on people's driveways the next morning, there, on the sports page, was a half-page picture of me with my name in the inscription below: "The Third Baseman tagged Matt Kunz out after rounding third." Needless to say, any hope I had of sports fame got off to a rocky start.

Thirteen years later, I was in the center of the House That Rockne Built, lined up on the Boston College 47-yard line in front of 80 thousand anxious football fans in Notre Dame Stadium. It was mid-season for a new head coach trying to turn things around after a poor start. Boston College had just scored to take the lead and momentum. Politics or no politics, I knew that the first string player had a bad knee and wasn't mobile. Although I wasn't recruited, the job had to get done, and I could move.

I ran out on the field deciding that they would have to take a TV timeout to get me back on the sidelines if they wanted to replace me with a lame player. I fully expected something to happen, but nothing did. I looked at Coach Meyer, Coach Davie, and Coach Doll, and no one was waving at me to get off the field. The referee blew the whistle, waved his arm in a big circular motion on the side of his body, and I thought, "Here we go. Game Time!"

Counting left to right, I had the "number four" player for Boston College's kickoff team. He was tall. He probably had four inches on me, and I had to make sure, whatever happened, that he was not going to be on the left hash mark when Allen Rossum caught the ball and made it to my level.

I watched the kicker to make sure he kicked the ball deep and didn't try anything like a short onside surprise. I wasn't going to make that same mistake again as I had in practice. Once I heard the thump and saw the ball going over my head, I ran to get back where I had to be and settled in position. My guy was running down the field exactly on the left hash looking at Rossum, and I was ready for a collision. I charged expecting impact and, to my surprise, he stopped. My momentum was great, but I tried to gather myself as I put my hands on his numbers. If I had tried to level him, I would have missed him. Instead I slipped trying to stay upright, but I managed to stay with him. I noticed his eyes. He wasn't looking at me. He tried to reach over me for some reason. I felt another hand on the back of my shoulder pads, and I gave a shove in the center of his numbers. It didn't knock him down, but it was enough.

I saw his head turn and his eyes look towards his own end zone. With the increasing roar of the crowd I knew that Rossum had broken through mid-field. In case Rossum was hit and fumbled, I left my assignment and gave chase. Rossum was 10 yards ahead of me dodging other BC players, but I ran after him anyway, leaping over a fallen BC player at mid-field. The crowd went nuts as he completed his 98-yard kickoff return for a touchdown and the lead. I ran with him into the end zone laughing and thinking how God must be smiling. On the sidelines I received several pats from my teammates, each of them congratulating all of us as we came off the field for taking back the lead. It was a tremendous feeling, yet due to politics it almost never happened.

I haven't been to the highest levels in sports, but I've seen just about all of them. I didn't play in the NFL, but my father did. I wasn't an All-American, but I've competed against many of them. I wasn't a National Champion, but I've played for coaches who've won four National Championships between them. I've participated in three Bowl Games, including the Orange Bowl. I wasn't highly recruited out of high school, but I've played at the highest level in Division I football. I didn't have the most size or speed, but coaches have argued over me in their team meetings. I've coached on a team that went 13 and 0, and I've coached on a team that went 0 and 10. I've given over 400 hours of private lessons for athletes ages 6 to 26. I've run football camps for over 100 players each, and ultimately developed a system for athletic progression on the field. I've also helped educate players on understanding the political system off the field, as well as on how to manage relationships throughout an athletic career.

I've seen coaches and board members get fired in draft rooms. As a player, I've been thrown off of a team, had to fight my way back on the team, and been resurrected to the travel squad in half a year's time. I've participated in games in Hawaii and Dublin, Ireland. I've had intense meetings with two head coaches in their offices. I've done up-downs on pavement. I've experienced serious injury and come back after I was told by a position coach to "Leave football and have a nice life." Twice I've had to impress a new head coach before each of my senior years, both in high school and college. I've felt depression and exhilaration. Most importantly, I've seen directly how God loves his children. I love sports, and football in particular. Nothing has come easily to me, which is exactly why I feel called to help every other athlete by sharing my experiences.

\* \* \*

No coach on the sideline has ever won a game. No coach on the sideline, during any game, has ever scored a touchdown, made a free throw, earned a run, pinned an opponent, made a tackle, kicked a goal, or scored any points. The fact is that a coach's record is only reflected in the success of his players.

That being said, a player's success highly depends on his performance within the system that is designed by the coach, the athletic organization, and the league. As an athlete, it is very important to understand this concept. The athlete depends on the coach to devise a winning strategy, while the coach depends on the athlete to perform within the framework of how the strategy has been practiced. Each needs the other to achieve success.

For you to be the best athlete you can be, you'll want to then focus on three areas. The first involves improving your specific performance in competition. The second involves making sure you are in a system that will give you the best opportunity to develop. The third involves making good relationship decisions when unusual situations present themselves.

This book will be divided into three parts that address each of these areas. The first underlines the concept of being a performer in the arena. Here you will comprehend exactly how to focus your energy into the three areas of Alignment, Rules, and Technique (ART), with the ultimate goal being your ability to play with confidence.

The second part helps you understand the politics surrounding sports. There is an ART to this as well. Most athletes don't realize how much understanding this piece to their puzzle makes a difference in whether or not they'll have a good experience and be able to develop.

The third part emphasizes managing relationships that surround you as an athlete. Anything that takes you away from your ART focus will limit your potential, and you need to manage those challenges that can come from being an athlete both on and off the field. Some relationships are good, while others can destroy your athletic future. Here I want to describe how some of those relationships can present themselves to you, and offer wisdom about how to know whether you are managing your relationships correctly.

This book is strictly for the athlete, but the coach who truly wants to see his players become the best well-rounded individuals he's ever been around will also benefit. Parents, too, can learn from this book, but they will have to see it through the eyes of the athlete. This book is definitely about winning, but winning comes from aligning ourselves with the way God made the world, and then enlisting the help of others to be a part of our success. Athletic competition forces us to use God's creation to the best of our abilities, or else we lose. In few other arenas can you see the completion of man's mind, body, and soul in God's creation. At the same time, sports don't just build character—they reveal it. When you are in the game, people will be able to see you exactly for what you are, and you cannot hide. That is the risk that those in sports take.

I believe that God uses the risk in sports as His tool to help us become all that we were meant to be in His creation. As athletes, we find out what it means to be alive with what we have been given. As players, we find out how we fit into this world that God created. It is my purpose to help you get the most out of your athletic career by providing you with the knowledge and wisdom that comes from experience.

Then, after you read this book, it is my hope that you will keep it as your guide. You should read it as a refresher after every season so that you can be better prepared for the next one. More than likely you will encounter a new experience each season, and you will need to remember some of the wisdom I hope to provide for you. Finally, after reading *Triumph!* remember to have fun, and go and Play with Confidence!

# PART I

## IT'S NOT A SCIENCE.
## IT'S AN ART.

# CHAPTER 1
## Player Frustration

**MY SENIOR YEAR IN HIGH SCHOOL,** I played offensive guard for our undermanned football team. Having been coached by my father, George Kunz, who was an eight-time pro-bowler and was twice rated the best offensive lineman in the NFL, I learned the technique to block properly. I had great success playing against defensive linemen who outweighed me by 80 pounds. One day, during a practice when the temperature was over 100 degrees in the Las Vegas heat, my father said, "Guys, we need to hit the sled. Now I'm not making you do it just because I want to. I know it's hot out. But we need to work on our timing because I want you to understand that blocking isn't a science. It's an art." After he said that, we worked diligently on our technique. It paid off because we were very competitive for a small school in the largest classification of football in our state. We had 27 guys on our varsity team playing against teams that had over 60 players each. One of us, our center Grey Ruegamer, even went on to a great career in the NFL and won two Super Bowl rings.

But as a sixteen-year-old high school junior, you don't always remember things your father says at the right time. Usually it goes in one ear and out the other, right? It's not always that you don't hear it. Sometimes, you just aren't aware of when to put it into practice. Knowing when to do these things is a part of wisdom that can only come with experience.

*   *   *

Flashing forward two years, I had arrived at Notre Dame as a walk-on football player. I was offered scholarships to a few smaller schools on the west coast, but I knew that Notre Dame was the place I wanted to be. Imagine my surprise when my position coach, Don Martingdale, came up to me and said, "Matt, here's your jersey. We're going to put you with the defensive backs." The what?! You mean you want to put me in a two-point stance and have me back-pedal? Did you forget I was a lineman? I thought, "You're the coach and you should know what you're doing, but I don't think it's going to be easy."

The first few days of practice proved my concerns. The guys they brought in were faster than I was. They had played the position and were All-Americans in high school. I was a decent size, but all this backpedaling was driving me crazy. I had gone forward for four years in high school, and now I don't even get to hit anybody. One day in fall practice, we had one-on-ones. When my turn came up, I lined up against Notre Dame's future All-American wide receiver Derrick Mays. The offensive coordinator, Dave Roberts, gave Derrick the signal to "Go Long", and at the snap he sprinted past me. I backpedaled like I was taught, turned my hips, stumbled, sprinted, and watched as Derrick caught a pass ten yards ahead of me. I wasn't even close.

When we went to watch film after practice, Dean Peas, our defensive backs coach, ran the film of me covering Derrick. While Derrick caught a beautifully thrown ball from quarterback Ron Powlus, the room was silent as the film showed me sprinting with all my might ten yards behind him. I had no chance whatsoever. Suddenly, one of the other defensive backs broke the silence by saying, "Good effort." I thought to myself, "I have got to change positions."

As time went on, I did change positions, first to scout team tight-end and a little offensive guard. I moved to defensive end a few weeks later, and finally found a place among the inside linebackers. There was no consistency, but I gave great effort based on how I thought the position should be played. The main frustration I had on the scout teams, though, was that I didn't get coaching. When I went with my inside linebacker position coaches to practice our position drills, I usually either had to play the part of the fullback or carry the ball for tackling drills. If by chance I did get to practice a drill, I only got one rep and could never perfect it.

One specific frustration I had came during tackling drills. I just never felt comfortable doing them. It's not that I was afraid of contact. It's that I always seemed to miss one of our shifty running backs in the open field, and as I made sure I just got ahold of him, he'd turn and try to run me over, knocking me backward. Perhaps I was thinking too much, but I was definitely doing something wrong.

One day after practice during my sophomore year, I thought to ask one of the coaches I got along with about my frustration. "Coach," I said. "I need you to tell me what I'm doing wrong. It seems like when I go in for a tackle against our shifty running backs, I always get knocked back. Now I know I'm just as big and as strong as these guys, but why does this seem to keep happening?"

"Well, Matt," he said. "When you get to the point where you can grab cloth, just hang on and wait for the rest of your teammates to help you. That's all you can do."

Now I loved and respected this coach, but I was very disappointed in his answer. He basically was telling me that I had no chance, that there was no physical way to tackle a shifty running back, and that I should just pray I could hang on long enough until one of my teammates came to my aid. This was a coach making a six-figure salary, coaching for a top-ten team, and the lesson was worthless. Thinking back to what my dad had said in the Las Vegas heat, I asked myself, "Where was the science? Where was the art?" I had been given neither, and I walked away frustrated.

\* \* \*

Years later, I was coaching one of my students in the ART of tackling. This was a private lesson for which I was hired. I had developed a reputation for coaching players beyond what seemed possible, and had begun a side business doing private football instruction.

"What's the most important part of tackling?" I asked him.

"I have to get there!" he said. He wisely remembered that nothing else mattered if he couldn't get to the ball carrier and do it the right way.

"Exactly," I said. "So the running back is running a sweep to the left sideline. What's your pursuit when he's sprinting?"

"I sprint with him two to three yards inside him. It's the East-West drill."

"Why are you inside him?" I asked.

"To prevent the cutback."

"Good. Why do you want to prevent the cutback?"

"Because he might score a touchdown," he said.

"Exactly! What tells you he may try to cut back?"

"Watch his shoulders. When they turn, he may be slowing down trying to cut back," he said.

"Good," I said. "What do you do when he slows? Do you just go for him?"

"No. I might miss him if I do. It now becomes the Box drill and I have to turn my hips and shuffle downhill under control."

"Good. What do you do if he decides he can't cut back and goes for the sideline again?"

"I'm back to the East-West drill," he said. "And I sprint to force him to the sideline where he'll run out of room."

"Great!" I said. "And how do you make the tackle?"

"Get my head across and make contact with the right shoulder."

"Which foot is in front?" I asked.

"Preferably my right. If it's my left I'm going to get run over." He learned this from experience.

"And what do you hit him with?"

"My shoulder?"

"Let me ask you again. What do you hit him with?" He needed to remember this.

"Oh yeah! My legs!" He remembered.

"Why?"

"The legs are the cannon, the body is the missile!" he said, referring to my lesson that the legs drive the body.

"Exactly!" I said. "And what do you do with your arms?"

"The legs drive him up, and the arms pull him down."

"Why?" I asked.

"It tears him apart, and he loses his balance." I had learned this from rugby because it's been my experience that rugby players know the physics of tackling better than anyone else.

"That's right!" I said. "So, do you ever go for the big hit?"

"Only if it's there. The big hits will come. And if I go for it when I'm not in position, I might miss him on the cutback or spin."

"Good. What should you be focused on, then?" I asked.

"Getting there in good position, using the field and my help properly, and making sure my feet are correct upon contact," he said.

"And..." I asked, making sure he remembered.

"And...Oh yeah! Hitting with my legs!" he said smiling.

"Do you ever use your head to make contact?" I asked.

"No." he said.

"Why?" I asked.

"Because it works better when I use my body. Plus, I don't want to hurt my neck," he said.

"Exactly. So, when you're in the Box drill, what are the three things a ball carrier can do to you?"

"He can run forward. He can cut back. And he can spin."

"What's your signal he's going forward?" I asked.

"He leans his shoulder forward."

"What about when he cuts or spins?"

"He plants hard to the outside. He also squares his shoulders if he tries to cut," he said.

"What's happening when he plants to cut or spin?" I asked.

"His momentum is changing, and he's vulnerable," he said rightly.

"Great! So, what do you do then?" I asked.

"Go get him! Inside-out!" he said.

"And if he keeps running East to West, what happens?" I asked.

"He goes out of bounds for no gain. We make the play and I don't even have to hit him," he said.

"Exactly!" I said. "You'll be using the field to your advantage, and you'll be increasing the odds of your success!" I patted him on the shoulder and told him that he was done for today. He had a successful lesson. As I walked back to my car, I knew that my client understood the science enough to put it together and make it an ART with his performance on the field. He was ready to play with confidence!

# BOX DRILL

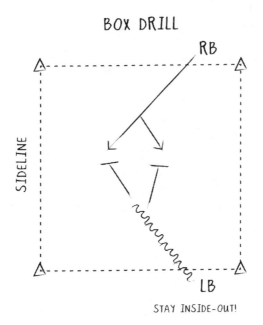

STAY INSIDE-OUT!

# EAST - WEST DRILL

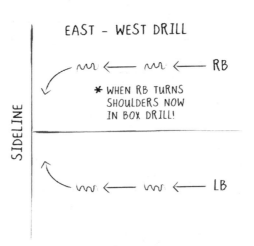

**✱ WHEN RB TURNS SHOULDERS NOW IN BOX DRILL!**

# CHAPTER 2

## You Are a Performer

"I WANT YOU TO UNDERSTAND that blocking isn't a science. It's an art," my father said that hot Las Vegas day. So, what's the difference between a science and an art? As I grew older and worked to understand many of the questions whose answers had eluded me in college, I began to pick up a lot of books. These were books about human kinetics, football, rugby, and running. I read science books about sports psychology and business books about team building and leadership. I read books about theology and Christian inspiration, trying to figure out how my experiences were a part of God's plan. I read each one thoroughly, underlining them all and asking more questions as I thought about my past experiences.

I remembered a time my freshman year at Notre Dame when my feet were right and I had a big hit on a Notre Dame tight-end who was seven inches taller than I was. I had knocked him off his feet, almost without any effort, and was so shocked that I had done this I tried to jump over him. I accidentally dug my cleats into the palm of his right hand as I tried to avoid hurting one of our starters. I remember overhearing one of my teammates on the sideline asking the others, "Did you see what Kunz just did?"

But I shook my head and asked myself, "How in the world did I just do that? He's a fifth-year senior and I'm a freshman. I'd like to be able to do this again, but I don't know how I did it in the first place!" Thinking about this experience and others like it, I dug into the books and put together the findings to get the answers.

The more I studied, the more I began to see how being an athlete incorporates the rules of physics. As I began to reflect, I could point to those times when I made a good play. Now I understand how I made those plays: I had everything working in alignment with the rules of physics. Likewise, I also reflected on those times when I could have made a play but didn't. Usually, those times happened because I didn't have the knowledge or understanding of how the rules of physics would help me in a situation, and some part of the situation was off which caused me to miss the play. Many times the coach didn't know enough of those physics to teach me why I had missed the play, and he instead decided to just yell or simply take me off the field while looking at me with disappointment.

The more I read, the more I began to understand science. Thinking back on what my father told me, I defined science as "an understanding of how God made the world." So being aware of the science of the world is the first step in being an athlete. If we throw a ball with X technique consistently, we can depend on it arriving in Y fashion. Gravity won't change. The ball will fall in exactly the same place if you throw it exactly the same way every time. Momentum works the same for everyone, and a certain effort is required to change its direction. Space is the same, and how we move in it in relation to each other can affect the way we pass the ball or be in position to make the tackle. Boundaries have an effect as well. They don't change in the arena, and we can use them to our advantage or let them be our disadvantage.

Understanding each of the sciences of the way God made the world is like adding a new arrow to your quiver. The more you figure out how to use the science to your advantage, the more you gain confidence in your ability to play within the world. Understanding the way the world works involves skill development, but it also involves your trained reaction to events and your instinct about why you are positioned where you are on the field.

So then, if playing sports isn't a science, but rather an art, what exactly is an "ART"? As I thought about this, I began to think of the great Italian artist and sculptor, Michelangelo. He spent years perfecting the craft of creating great art, but he went the extra mile. Upon reading *The Agony and the Ecstasy*, I discovered that he was so determined to understand the design of the human body that he broke into a morgue to dissect some corpses to see what was under the skin. This was at a time when it was a serious taboo to mess with human bodies. However, that did not deter him. He needed to know God's design to put it all together.

What he discovered allowed him to sculpt the great David and his Pietà. He also used his science to paint the ceiling of the Sistine Chapel at the Vatican. I've seen the ceiling of the Sistine Chapel and his Pietà in person at the Vatican, and the details of the human bodies that he put together in these works of art are absolutely amazing. The reason why he was able to do this was that he knew what was under the skin. So while I was thinking of Michelangelo, I thought to myself, "If a science is an understanding of the way God made the world, then an ART is putting together that science to make a thing of beauty."

## SCIENCE - PHYSICS OF HOW GOD MADE THE WORLD

## ART - PUTTING TOGETHER THE SCIENCE TO MAKE A THING OF BEAUTY

As I continued coaching, and getting into doing private lessons, I would explain this concept to my players. They understood it as I told them the story of how I put this into action. However, remembering it in practice is one thing; using it in the controlled chaos of a game is another. I wanted them to have a simple formula they could remember in the pressure of a tie ballgame. What will they be thinking about with a minute left in regulation? Will it be all their aches and pains? Will it be the noise from screaming fans and yelling coaches? Will they be afraid of their opponent? Will they just be thinking about how exhausted they are?

If you as the athlete think about any of these things, and not about what you are supposed to do, you run the risk of not making the play. Thus, I created an acronym for "ART." *A* is for Alignment. *R* is for Rules. *T* is for Technique.

# ALIGNMENT

# RULES

# TECHNIQUE

One of the great advantages of the ART for sports concept is that you can self-coach. When you are on the field, people are yelling in the stands, coaches are shouting from the sideline, your opponent is talking smack, and the energy level is high because the game is tied with 90 seconds to go. The best players are able to think for themselves on the field under the pressure of these circumstances. You can simply ask yourself three questions to build confidence after a good play, or, if you make a mistake, to determine what went wrong after a bad play so that you can correct it.

The first question is, "Was I properly Aligned?" If not, you will need to coach yourself to get back in Alignment to best use your space. If you were Aligned, then go to the second question, which is, "Did I follow my Rules?" If you didn't, simply remember your Rules for the play and be sure to follow them. If you are confident you followed your Rules, then move to the third question, which asks, "What was my Technique?" If you were in the right Alignment, and you followed your Rules, you might need to make sure you used your body to move appropriately to best your opponent, which is all Technique.

Let's get into understanding these in greater detail.

# CHAPTER 3

## *A* is for Alignment

**IT WAS LIKE A SCENE OUT OF** the movie *Braveheart*. The sky was cloudy with rain coming down. It was good old Scottish weather—only we weren't in Scotland. We were in the Atlanta area in November. The field was muddy and there was a steady chill in the air. Players from all around the world congregated on this field today. One short player with a shaved head and an accent I didn't recognize began to stare onto the field and psych himself into a frenzy. He said something in another language that sounded intense, reached into his mouth, and pulled out his teeth, which he promptly put into his bag for safe-keeping. "Yes," I thought. "This is definitely my first rugby game."

The game was intense and the action didn't stop. Since it was my first game, I knew what was going on about half the time. Practice helped, but the speed of competition made the situations change so quickly that by the time I knew what was going on, something else was happening. I knew I couldn't know it all, but if I could just try to be in the right spot and run in the right direction, I would at least help give my team a chance.

As it would happen, one of my teammates passed the ball to me, and I ran toward the defense. One of the defenders was on me right away, and I had no way to get past him. I knew I'd have to get rid of the ball, so in an instant I passed the ball to my right without so much as taking a look to make sure my teammate was there. It was all on trust. There was no time to look. The defender put his shoulder into my chest and drove me into the ground. The air was knocked out of me, and I struggled to get up. Realizing that the game didn't stop and wasn't going to stop even if I couldn't breathe, I came back to my feet and tried to get back in proper Alignment.

Fortunately, when I passed that ball, my teammate was in the right place. He stayed Aligned to my position exactly as we had practiced, and he was right where he should have been when I passed him the ball. He made a move and drove the ball deeper into our opponent's field, where we scored a try and eventually won the game. Had he not been Aligned to my position as he was, the ball might have hit the ground with an opportunity for the other team to win the game.

To understand Alignment, you need to ask yourself, "Where am I when the play begins?" If you play soccer, do you know why your coach has lined you up where he has on a corner kick? If you play football, do you know why your coach has put you exactly where he has at the beginning of the play? If you wrestle, do you know where you need to be in relation to your opponent to get a proper takedown? If you play basketball, do you know where you should be as the point guard brings the ball up the court? If you play baseball, do you listen to your scouting reports and change your Alignment when certain batters come up to bat based on where they usually hit the ball?

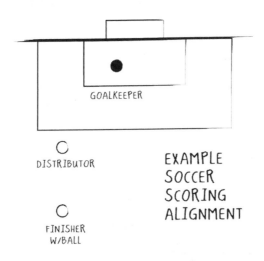

GOALKEEPER

DISTRIBUTOR

FINISHER
W/BALL

EXAMPLE
SOCCER
SCORING
ALIGNMENT

Asking where you are supposed to be or "What is my Alignment?" before the play begins helps you in the physics of space. You can have great Technique and follow your Rules exactly, but if you aren't in the right spot, you are not going to execute the play properly. This is important because controlling your space, whether in a team or individual sport, gives you a great opportunity to control the ball and your opponent. If you are on defense and you can't control your space when the ball is near you, there will be a breakdown in the defense and the offense will have an opportunity to score. If you are on offense and you effectively use your space, you put pressure on the defense and give your team a great chance to get points on the board.

Today's game of football has become very space conscious. As teams with smaller players try to compete with teams that are more established, coaches have adopted offensive plays in a system they call "The Spread." The idea at first was to take as much advantage as possible of the space in the open field so that smaller players might have a chance to get around bigger players who haven't practiced moving in space. As the system caught on, the more established teams, including those in the National Football League, began to base their offenses on the "space in open field" concept. Now that the system has gained popularity, defenses have changed to the point where they play more defensive backs per down. They need personnel on the field who are adept at moving in space, and they are Aligned on the field prior to the ball being snapped so that they might take away the space advantage of the offense.

In just about every sport the advantage goes to the offense because they know where they are going with the ball. The defense has to react. But with the proper use of space, the defense can regain that advantage and use the field to trap the offense, force a bad play, and get the ball back. The defensive players won't have a good chance at doing this if they don't first get into Alignment to utilize their space.

Likewise, the offense can find those breakdowns in space and use those opportunities to get past the defense. Offensive coaches look for spacing opportunities all the time, and that is why they determine where each player needs to be Aligned before the designed play begins. This is also why offensive coaches move players before a play happens. They want to get defensive players out of their Alignment. This is why you need to be conscious of your Alignment at the beginning of each play, both offensively and defensively.

Great players understand how to use great spacing to their advantage. They exercise diligently in the off-season so that as the game wears on they can focus on where they need to be instead of worrying about their legs not getting them to the right spot. Running is very important to maintaining proper spacing, as most fields of play are rather large. The best players, however, know that if they begin the play by being properly Aligned, they use less energy, they force their opponent to work harder, and they have a great chance at achieving a victory when the clock runs out.

Take a few moments to reflect on your plays, and ask yourself if you understand exactly where you need to be Aligned when the play begins. Many times your Alignment will be a spot on the court or field. Other times your Alignment will be in relation to one of your teammates, as my teammate was in the rugby game. If you are on defense, your Alignment might be in relation to where an offensive player is, where your defensive teammates are, or a combination of both. You need to understand where you begin so that you can end with a successful play.

# CHAPTER 4

## *R* is for Rules

**I LOVED WATCHING A COMMERCIAL** during the basketball season that showed a young rookie Michael Jordan playing a pickup game against himself, the older, more experienced Michael Jordan as he was nearing retirement. The two went back and forth, and on one play, the young Jordan said boastfully, "I could have dunked it." Replying immediately, the wiser Jordan said, "You *should* have dunked it."

Have you ever watched a basketball game and seen a pass to a player, except that the receiving player wasn't there to receive it? In the game of football, TV announcers have a phrase for when a quarterback throws a pass to a wide receiver, but the wide receiver goes a different way. They say, "Those two weren't on the same page." Often times a quarterback is sacked just because no one was there to block the defender. Why didn't one of those big linemen pick him up, or did the running back miss his assignment? What about in soccer when a defender lets a forward get a free shot at the goal? How could he let that happen? How could a young baseball player rounding third get tagged out when he thought he could score, as happened to me? It's quite simple, actually. These situations occur because the players missed the second part of the ART concept: Rules.

When I discuss Rules with my clients, I'm not talking about the rules in terms of what a referee judges. I'm talking about strategy. Once again, if you are Aligned properly, and you have great Technique, but you zigged when you should have zagged, you're not going to be in position to make the play. Worse yet, you won't look very good on the field.

I have found that the Rules area of the ART concept is really lacking among players. I directly link this to coaching. It's like the football coach who told me to grab and hang on during tackling drills. I realized later that I had good spacing, and I eventually did get proper Technique. However, the shiftiness of the running back drove me nuts. This is because no one explained the Rules of how to control his shiftiness within the space of the drill.

So, if coaching is the problem, why is this so? I think the reason why is that it can be very complicated for a coach to know exactly what every player should be doing on every single play in every single situation before a play even starts. Take an offensive line coach of a youth football team, for example. He has to teach a set of Rules for 20 different plays for five different players. That's over 100 Rules to be responsible for, and he's just an unpaid volunteer assistant coach!

Because of this complexity, the best coaches simplify the Rules for their players. That offensive line coach might teach his players the most consistent rule that they will each have on most offensive plays, such as "Gap, Down, Backer." The Rule works like this. The offensive tackle, for example, looks to his inside towards the center. If there is a defender there in the "Gap," he blocks him. If there is no one there, he looks past the Gap to help the center and he blocks "Down" to him. If there is no one there, he looks for a linebacker or "Backer." If there is a linebacker, he blocks him. Thus, the offensive tackle follows his Rule for the play.

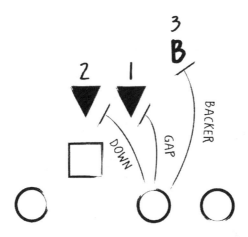

# FOOTBALL "GAP-DOWN-BACKER" RULES

When I was playing on the offensive line and I had a question about who to block, my father would respond back to me, "What's your rule?" He wanted me to understand how to think on the field, and going back to the Rules gave me confidence as to what was my responsibility. As I coached linebackers in high school, I also made sure that my players had their Rules. However, unlike the offensive players whose Rules were mostly designed based on the advantage of knowing where they were going, the defensive Rules were designed to help them react more quickly to what the offensive player was doing.

I hammered home the Rules for my linebackers on a regular basis. After they had their Alignment, I often asked them what they should be looking at. Should they be distracted by the entire atmosphere, the fans, and the cheerleaders? Of course not! Yet most of them had never thought of that, and if they weren't focused on the right thing, they might get lazy and focus on the wrong things.

My players were quickly taught to be looking at the forehead of the running back closest to them. If that helmet went left, I wanted their Rule to be that their first step would be left. If that helmet went right, I wanted their Rule to be that their first step would be to their right. It was simple, but their Rules helped them maintain their Alignment advantage.

The same holds true for soccer. Offensive Rules for a particular play might be to fake a pass left and get the defender off her balance before passing the ball to an open teammate on her right. Defensive Rules involve getting back in Alignment immediately, focusing on the ball handler's waist line with an inside Alignment between the ball and the goalie. It's all a choreographed performance, and when the next situation arrives, following the Rules keeps a player in position to help her team.

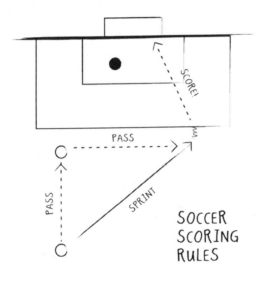

SOCCER
SCORING
RULES

A team whose players all understand their Rules is a formidable force. These teams work together in a beautiful choreography as each of them works his assignment. On the other hand, a team that has a player or two who doesn't know his Rules is a disaster. As a defensive coordinator, I am still upset about a defensive cornerback that didn't come to practice leading up to an important playoff game. I had worked diligently all week making sure that my players knew exactly what to do in every situation that they should expect to see. Ten of my players were ready, but the one who missed practice decided to show up only for game day. Unfortunately, the league rules said I had to play him even though he went rogue for the week.

We were winning the game 6-0 late in the third quarter, and in desperation, the other team lined up for their trick play that was going to my cornerback. I saw it coming, but sure enough, he didn't do what I had told his replacement all week long, and he bit on the fake and they scored. The score was now tied, 6-6.

This had an effect on my safety. He felt that the cornerback was now unreliable because he should have known his Rules on that play. My safety felt he had to compensate for the cornerback. Sure enough, the other team had a fake for the safety, and his overcompensation led to their go-ahead touchdown in the fourth quarter. My safety didn't follow his own Rules, and we lost 6-12. I should have seen the safety overcompensating and made sure he stuck with his ART concept. Because I didn't see it happening, we lost the game.

To understand the Rules, a player needs to have good communication with the coach. The coach should teach, the player should listen, and then the player should give feedback to the coach. If the player does not understand what the coach is telling him, one of the best things he can do is ask, "Coach, what is my Rule on this play?" This tells the coach that he needs to simplify his teaching. He may be speaking in concepts because he likes to talk. Simplifying, he should tell the player something like, "If your opponent does this, then I want you to do that. If your opponent doesn't do this, then I want you to do this other thing instead." Simplifying Rules for players lets them act and react far more effectively.

In the late 1980s, the Kansas City Chiefs had a large bruising tailback named Christian Okoye. I remember one particular offensive possession on Monday Night Football when Okoye was responsible for every yard of an opening touchdown drive. He was an amazing player. What was interesting, though, was his story when he first decided to play football in college. He had come to America from Africa, and he wanted to play football. However, he didn't know the Rules as they applied in the ART concept. According to the TV announcers in the game, his coaches cut out footprints and laid them in the direction he was supposed to run. These footprints became his visual to know "If this, then do that." From these humble beginnings, Okoye earned the NFL league rushing title in 1989 and had two Pro-Bowl appearances.

The bottom line is this. All members of a team are responsible for knowing what they are supposed to do in all situations. A coach has the complicated job of anticipating situations, designing Rules for each player in those situations, and then communicating the Rules to each player so that they can execute on the field. When practicing, it's important to remember that small steps in the right direction are far faster than any big steps in the wrong direction. Coaches and players need to focus on taking those right steps. Once the players are in the game, however, they have to execute their Rules on their own. If they can do this, then they move their ART concept toward operating their bodies physically through the proper use of physics, which we call Technique.

# CHAPTER 5

## *T* is for Technique

**AS A SOPHOMORE SPECIAL TEAMS** player at Notre Dame, I was often selected to line up on the scout team against the first and second team punt teams directly in front of the long snapper. We had two long snappers at that time, and they were both very good. However, between the two, it was Ryan Leahy that always frustrated me the most. I had a decent get-off, watching a part of the ball for any movement that would signal my get-off to rush the punter. However, I could never understand why it was that Leahy would always get me. It wasn't particularly size or speed, but he was an upperclassman, and he understood the importance of having great Technique. He knew that if he moved exactly as he was supposed to, exactly as Coach Joe Moore trained him, he would increase his chances of being in position to make the play more times than not. By using the physics of the world around him, Ryan Leahy became an All-American.

Just as being in the right place (Alignment) and doing the right thing (Rules) can separate an athlete from the rest of the pack, the rubber meets the road only if the athlete can protect himself on the field of play. This is where Technique comes in to play. If a player can't protect himself on the field, he can be Aligned perfectly and follow his Rules exactly, but he won't make the play. Fortunately, and against the thought processes of many coaches out there, every athlete can learn the Technique that will help him win on the field. In fact, knowing Technique along with his Alignment and Rules will give the athlete greater confidence than an opponent who might be bigger and stronger than every player on the field but has no idea where he is going.

Fortunately, for every sport, there is usually just one thing a player needs to excel at in order to gain confidence in everything else. In football, for example, it's hitting. Think about it. Linemen won't block, running backs won't break tackles, defensive players won't tackle, and quarterbacks will feel vulnerable if they think that every time they come into contact with another player they are going to get hurt. They have to feel that they can protect themselves on every play, and the only way to do that is to learn how to hit. Once they learn how to hit, they then get proficient at tackling, blocking, running, throwing, and everything in between because they know that they can protect themselves.

Soccer is a different sport altogether, but I would say that there is just one thing a player should feel comfortable with in order to gain confidence in all the other skills, and that is controlling a soccer ball with her feet in her own space. She has to feel confident that she can control the ball when it's near her before she can feel confident enough to pass it between defenders to someone else. It's embarrassing to lose a ball to an opponent when you're on the field in front of friends and fans, and if a player can't feel confident enough to handle the basics, how will she gain the confidence needed to handle everything else?

I would also say basketball is similar to soccer. Before a player can learn confidence in shooting, rebounding, or passing, he has to learn how to dribble the ball. If he can't dribble the ball, he can't move, and not being able to move might put him at risk of being surrounded, making it even harder to pass the ball.

In baseball, before hitting and throwing, I would say a player needs to feel confident in his ability to catch before anything else. Everyone strikes out, and an errant throw might be embarrassing, but not being able to catch a ball will hurt. When your mechanics of catching become automatic, then you focus on the mechanics of throwing. Once throwing is automatic, you focus on batting.

Other sports also have one thing that all athletes need to know before they can learn everything else. Wrestlers should learn a "neck bridge." Tennis players should be confident that they can hit the ball with the racket. Lacrosse players need to be able to run with the ball. Swimmers need to be able to breathe while performing their stroke.

As I coached my athletes in the primary Technique, I realized that I had to train their thought processes not to fight the way their body is made. Too often, I would get kids who felt that they had to get a big hit, so they would throw their shoulder, and then wonder why they would get hurt or knocked off balance. Other kids would come running in like a freight train, trying with all their might to hit a simple dummy, only to be disappointed that they missed the bag entirely or that they didn't get the impact that they were expecting.

After an attempt or two with the same results, I would settle the athlete down and have him look around. "It's a big field out there, isn't it?" He would agree. He'd see a lot of green. I'd then ask him what he thought of those big trees on the other side of the fence. He'd look puzzled and say that they were big and green.

"Exactly," I'd say. "Are they trying to be anything other than big and green?"

"No," he'd say.

"Correct! They are being and doing exactly what they are supposed to do in their environment, right?" He'd nod his head in agreement. "And, what do you think about that bird flying in the air?" I'd continue. "He seems to make it look pretty easy, doesn't he?" My student would also agree to this.

"Let me ask another question," I'd continue. "If you wanted to swim across a river, would it be easier to swim against the current or with it?"

"Obviously, you'd want to swim with it," he'd say.

"Great!" I'd exclaim. "So, with God having made all this nature to work exactly as it should, wouldn't you also want to work your body exactly as it should? And if you did, wouldn't it be easy, like a person swimming with the current or a bird flying through the air?"

"Yes," he'd respond, knowing where I was going but not believing me.

Then I'd explain to him that the rules of physics apply as much to him and his play on the field as they do to all of the nature that he sees around him. Gravity is the same today as it was 5000 years ago. A force operates the same today as it will 5000 years from now. Unlike nature, though, we have the choice to use the science of physics to our benefit, or to go against it to our detriment. It's that choice that separates us and decides who we are at our core. In sports, we can choose to do it our way, or we can choose to respect how things were created and make things easy on ourselves. Are we humble about our existence, or are we not?

What's frustrating for me is that so many times coaches, some of whom are well meaning, push or scare kids to force a play rather than teaching them how to let the play come to them. The best coaches I've been around have always understood those simple rules of physics, taught Techniques that utilize those rules, and then would get all over their players if they ever deviated from those Techniques. These coaches don't de-emphasize effort. On the contrary, they demand tremendous effort to follow the ART of the game. What's fascinating is that their players, who let the plays come to them, tend to make more big plays. They know that misdirected effort is wasted effort. Again, small steps in the right direction are better than any big step in the wrong direction.

As a football coach at practice, I would often know if a player was going to make his assignment before impact simply by the way his feet lined up when he approached. If he was run over on impact, I would go to him and ask him why he thought that happened while also asking him if getting run over felt good. If he didn't know why it happened, I would ask him how his feet were on impact. If he didn't know, then I would know that he wasn't self-correcting, and he might be a liability on the field during a game.

On the other end of the spectrum, time after time, I loved seeing the joy on my athletes' faces when they finally "Got it!" It always seemed to happen the same way, too.

During my lessons, I would often have the athlete's dad hold an arm dummy as we went over hitting Technique. Initial efforts to hit often made barely a sound, and the dad would never move. The dad would try to offer encouragement, and the student would seem to get frustrated. Simply and slowly, however, I would help the student understand how he should approach and then use his legs to drive the impact, relaxing his shoulders and torso while keeping his back straight. He needed to have his right foot in front if he was making contact with the right shoulder, and his left foot in front if he was making contact with his left shoulder. He needed to trust that his legs would have enough power to drive impact through his torso.

Step by step, the athlete would learn the basics … until it happened. With his back straight and his forearm relaxed in front of him, he would power his legs right into the arm dummy with such force that you could hear a solid "POP!" The jolt would knock the dad back as his son's force rocked his dad's insides and his dad's neck made a whiplash motion. Then, I couldn't help but smile at the irony when the dad would exclaim, "That was GREAT!" He didn't realize it, but Dad was going to need to see his chiropractor tomorrow.

What was more amazing was watching the student's reaction. "I hardly felt anything!" they would say. And they'd be right. Using their body the way it was designed allowed them to distribute so much power without feeling any of the negative effects of the jolt. It's the same thing I felt when I knocked over that large Notre Dame tight end in practice, but didn't know how I did it. I've seen this experience happen over and over again with football players ages 6 to 26. Once they "got it" they had the confidence to continue learning.

The key to understanding any sport's primary Technique is twofold. First, understand the proper physics of the motion. Know why you are doing what you are doing. This is important, because if you don't believe in it, you will gravitate back towards that motion that didn't work, and you'll only get more frustrated.

Second, practice the motion over and over and over again until you commit the motion to muscle memory. Your mind has to comprehend what the motion is instantaneously in the field of play, and how well you react in game situations depends on how well your muscle memory is trained. There is no way around it. You're going to have to practice the basic motion of the primary Technique each day if you want to be consistent at the ART concept. For example, recently I inquired about learning judo. In my discussions, I found out that many of the judo throws had to be performed 1000 times before you can even test to get a new belt. Fortunately, the more you practice it, the easier it feels.

Let me give you one more story to emphasize my point. While I was in high school and college, I ran a lot. I would run just about every other day to make sure I was in shape to get ready to compete. Unfortunately, I had no idea how to run. I always felt like my gears were going, but I never felt at ease while running. It was an effort. I didn't mind the effort, but as competition got tougher, I never felt I could get past fourth gear. My best 40-time was just under 4.8 seconds, when it needed to be well under 4.7.

Unfortunately, I let my college career end without ever really grasping the proper mechanics of sprinting. Sure, I did all the drills and strapped on all those parachutes in college, but something was missing.

A couple of years after college, I spent a summer in south Georgia. There wasn't much to do down there after work, so I decided to see if I could answer all those questions I had from when I was playing football, including why I never felt at ease while running while so many of my teammates had. I wasn't going to accept the usual coaching mantra that some things are just the way they are, and you either have it or you don't. There had to be a way.

While searching for knowledge, I found a book written by Dr. Michael Yessis called *Explosive Running*. Immediately, I began to pore over it. After working out at a local gym, I took my book with me to a high school football field and began doing the drills outlined in that book while understanding why I was doing what I was doing. I admit it felt funny to do single leg jumps while not wearing any shoes with all the local residents staring at me. Still, I was determined to get to the answer.

After a few weeks, I noticed that the motions I was performing felt less awkward. As I tried to put together the motions into a sprinting form, I felt as I had when I had first ridden a bicycle, a little wobbly but somewhat more at ease. Finally, after just a few weeks of gaining my new muscle memory, I felt like I was driving a new car while I was running, and I was finally in fifth gear!

Shortly after I felt I had a grasp of it, I ran into two other athletes who were on the field throwing a football around. One of them was a wide receiver who was about to leave in a few weeks to work out with a Canadian football team. This is my chance, I thought, and I offered to play defense against him while he ran his routes. He was one of those shifty wide receivers who loved to fake before breaking on his route, just like those shifty running backs in my college tackling drills. I never could have covered those guys in college. However, to my surprise, I had him covered pretty much lockstep. Plus, I felt at ease! After the drill, the wide receiver said, "That was good coverage. Very good coverage." I had to laugh, as no one had ever said that to me in eight years of football. Now I was covering a future pro!

A few weeks later, I moved back to Atlanta and joined a couple of sports teams. During a men's softball game, I grounded a ball to the shortstop, which in the past would have made me an easy out. However, I remember hearing my teammates gasp in amazement as they watched me sprint and beat the throw to first base. Unfortunately, I decided to show off by stealing second, and with my new speed I hadn't learned how to stop. I overran second base, and the opposition tagged me out. The Technique was great, but I should have followed my Rules.

As previously mentioned, I also played rugby when I made it back to Atlanta. Normally a club team would place me where the slower rugged players lined up near the scrum. I was astonished when they wanted me where the speed guys were. Speed in sports is a special thing, and to be included in that category during that time still amazes me. However, it all began with my willingness to submit to the physics of proper running motion. Once I learned why I needed to use the proper running Technique, applying the ART concept in my own games helped me compete at higher levels with less effort.

One more thing I feel I should mention. Whenever I was coaching my athletes, I never asked them to do anything that I didn't at one time or another have to do myself. I developed each of these principles from personal experience during my own sports training to make sure they worked, and then I was better able to communicate these processes to my players. In my mind, there is no greater communication than when the message comes from the heart of experience. For you coaches and team captains who wish to motivate, enthusiastic belief in truth will win more hearts over everything else. Remember that!

# CHAPTER 6
## Just Do It Right

**IT WAS A SUNNY COOL SATURDAY** in the park, the day after Halloween. Our football team was undefeated, but we were up against the only other undefeated team in the league. For a game like this, more fans, more enthusiasm, and more intensity surround the field, and all the fans and parents were excited for the game.

When the game went underway, the intensity didn't disappoint. The other team made two big plays early on and scored two touchdowns to take a 12-0 lead. Our team seemed in a daze. I think many of the kids went out trick-or-treating the night before even though we advised them that doing so wouldn't be a good idea.

Fortunately, the fact that our team was losing for the first time this season seemed to wake them up, and the hitting intensified. The game became a struggle, with every athlete battling to gain an advantage. Our team managed to score in the third quarter, and with time running out, our quarterback ran the ball down the left sideline on a broken play into the end zone. Touchdown! The game was tied 12-12 and we were going into overtime.

Our opponents received the ball to start the overtime period, but our defense played well enough to stop them and our offense took control. Play after play, we drove the ball towards their end zone. Listening to the fans and the coaches on the other side of the field, I waited for the proverbial phrase that would come when a team is getting beat. Sure enough, the phrase was shouted by our opponent's assistant coach as well as a dad leaning over the chain link fence. "Come on, guys! Suck it up!" When I heard that, I knew we had them. We ran the ball a few more times and won the game 18-12. It was a win that solidified our undefeated season and propelled us to the championship.

How many times will an athlete hear from his coach or parents to "suck it up in the fourth quarter!" During the course of a season, I would estimate that a typical athlete hears this phrase over 20 or 30 times. However, as I coached my players, I wanted them to think differently. I never de-emphasized effort. However, if they had to "suck it up in the fourth quarter," then they weren't doing things right. Instead, I told them, "Just do it right. Make the other team 'suck it up' in the fourth quarter after you've worn them down. I'd rather you have fun and win the game!"

This is why I can't emphasize enough the ART concept for sports. Players who review this simple checklist between plays, regardless of ability, increase so much in confidence that they excel well beyond what they themselves ever thought they were capable of. As I've done my own private coaching, I've had a seventh grader start for his eighth grade football team. I've had an undersized lineman start as an offensive guard for his AAAAA football team. I've had a player who had never played before start his season as quarterback and inside linebacker. This same player was later moved to tight-end where he caught the game-winning pass for his championship game.

I've helped the smallest player in his league start for his team. I've helped those who were drafted last in their league make the All-Star Team. I've helped a freshman football team, who as eighth graders didn't win a single game and would lose by an average of over 30 points per game, become competitive by winning two games and reduce their margin of loss to the low single digits. This same team would go on to win the AAAA State Championship in Georgia as high school seniors. Finally, I've helped an undersized defensive back earn recognition as Defensive Player of the Year for his AAAAA high school football team.

There are countless other stories of success with this concept that I can relate to you, and each one is amazing. As I dealt with more clients, it happened so frequently that I stopped being surprised. I knew it was only a matter of time before that special moment of achievement would be reached.

However, what is more amazing is how many coaches refuse to develop the potential created inside each and every one of their players. As an athlete or parent, if all you need to be concerned about is the ART concept, the game would be easy. Unfortunately, that is not reality, and the next struggle you will face is how to deal with the politics of sports. We'll go into that in detail next.

# PART II

## SPORTS POLITICS

# CHAPTER 7
## The Sports System

I WAS RECENTLY TALKING with a friend of mine whose son was playing soccer, but had decided to try out for football. As a two-sport athlete, his son was going to play both sports during the same season since practice time didn't conflict. As a soccer player, he'd had a poor experience with a coach in a particular league the prior year. However, the parent had chosen not to ask around to see if there were any alternative programs. The next fall, the player wound up being back on the same team with the same coach and is now having the same experience.

However, when it came to football, the parent did his homework. He asked around to find out which football program was the best in the area. He looked at fields to see if they were maintained. He interviewed parents whose sons already played football. Finally, he selected what he determined would be the best program and signed his son up for football. His son is having a great experience at football, but is wondering why his soccer experience is so horrible. As we talked, I asked him again if his son played for the same coach last year. He said he did, but he realized where I was going. I asked him if he really then expected anything different,

and he had to admit that he didn't put the same effort into selecting a soccer team that he did a football team. He also admitted
that the players were picking up bad habits on the field. Realizing
his situation, he now understands that the only way to correct the
soccer situation is to find training outside of soccer practice, and to
encourage his son to be a team player. His son should also encourage his teammates in this bad situation. Unfortunately, to receive
additional training requires money, and he wishes he had talked
with me beforehand.

Perhaps it's the system. Perhaps coaches don't feel they can
develop every player on a 100-man football team, for example, so
they only work with the top 20% using the 80-20 Pareto Principle.
Perhaps it's the pressure to win from the administration or the local
booster club, so they think they should only play those players who
look good in their uniforms with muscles bulging, even though they
can't remember their assignments. Perhaps they play one player
over another because a booster gave the coach some money under
the table. Perhaps they recruit outside the district, giving up on
the resident team's development in order to bring in "Top Talent."
Perhaps it's a professional team owner who doesn't really understand his sport. However, because he has money and because he
believes one player is better than he really is, he forces his coach to
start him over someone who is better.

Over the years, my family and I have seen it all when it comes to
the politics of sports. My father went through it as an NFL player,
and he is still going through it with the Hall of Fame process. I saw
it in high school, and I was personally affected by it as a player at
Notre Dame. As I coached I couldn't believe my eyes when I saw
how grown-ups played politics in order to serve themselves. What
happens off the field affects what happens on the field, so as a player,
or a parent, it's important to know how to handle the events that
will transpire during the course of an athlete's career. Also, how
well you handle the politics of sports may very well determine the
length of your career as an athlete.

To begin with, what is politics? First, I should clarify the difference
between what I mean by relationships and politics. Relationships
are defined by your personal thoughts, feelings, and interactions

with one or more people. Politics is when those thoughts, feelings, and interactions with other people are influenced by a third party.

I'll use a couple of simple examples to make my point. Let's say Jane doesn't like Lisa. It's not a good relationship. Why doesn't Jane like Lisa? Well, everyone knows that Jane and Lisa both like Bob. Even though Bob doesn't like either of them and likes Katie instead, he is influencing the thoughts, feelings, and interactions between Jane and Lisa. That's politics.

Let's say Tracy wants to become friends with Katie. She doesn't "like" Bob, but because Bob is popular, she wants to become friends with Katie so she can become popular also. Tracy's relationship with Katie is also influenced by Bob, but in a different way. This, too, is not a good relationship. It's politics.

Having a good relationship is very simple. Remove the third party influence from those thoughts, feelings, and interactions. The more positive relationships you have around you, the less your Athletic career will be determined by politics. It is very simple. Note that I didn't say "easy." I said "simple." There's a difference.

Let's get into it.

## Sports Organizational Structure

I remember what it was like showing up to the elementary school for T-ball signups. I was nervous. Hey, what six year-old wouldn't be? There were all these adults standing around tables, and forms, and lines. I brought my baseball glove, and I realized once we were inside that I didn't need it. Hats and jerseys were handed out. Dad shook hands with all the other adults. It was like they were all part of some secret club, some structure that had all the power to dictate my future.

When practices began, I forgot all about the adults at signups. However, what I came to realize later was that those adults in that elementary school room, and all the other rooms I was a part of later, were responsible for the success of the league and teams. As I also came to understand later, when the adults acted like adults, the league or team was successful. When those adults began to act like children, things got hairy.

So, how is a sports organization structured? Let's say that you are in the middle of your season. By now, you know that you report directly to your position coach, who is more commonly known as an assistant coach. Your assistant coach is responsible for teaching a certain set of skills to a group of players, preferably using the ART concept. He also has a say in which players are most reliable, which players should see playing time on the field, and who should replace them when they need to come off the field. This process is what's known as creating a depth chart. When the season is over, a good assistant coach will have retained his best players to come back next season, and will have also attracted more players to want to join them. This is a process called "recruiting."

Your assistant coach takes direction from your head coach. Often, head and assistant coaches meet regularly months before your season starts. They often decide what skills they want their players to have, which players they should draft, which players they want to avoid in the draft, what strategy they will employ against the other teams, and how they are going to teach the necessary skills to their players.

Ultimately, the success of a team comes down to a head coach. Often a head coach plays both the roles of head coach and assistant coach, but all the other assistant coaches report to the head coach. As a player, you will quickly understand that your head coach must make sure you know how to protect yourself on the field, understand your Rules, and line up correctly. Does this sound familiar? Also, the head coach has the final say on the depth chart and strategy. Of course, a head coach will help retain and develop current players, but will also work to "recruit" additional players to come and join the team. As a player, you've probably seen and understood many of these things already. However, you're not done yet. What we've just gone over is only the tip of the iceberg.

The head coach also has parent organizations reporting to him. Usually a team mom or team dad leads a group of parents in youth organizations to help with things such as travel arrangements, snacks, water, trophies, uniforms, equipment, and sports injuries. As you get further into high school and college, many of these duties are taken over by hired personnel, such as a head trainer, a strength trainer, or a head equipment manager, but the remaining duties are performed by a parent booster club. A parent booster club helps organize the parents for fundraising, for setting up pre-game meals, and for throwing the end-of-season party. These parent organizations should take their direction from the head coach and athletic director to do all that is required to help the team be successful. If the team is successful, everybody wins. Where it gets crazy is when parents or boosters use these positions to influence the head coach. Remember what I said about relationships being influenced by a third party? That's right, it then becomes political. We'll talk more about this later.

Now, the head coach doesn't have supreme power. Players may think he does because he has a lot of power over the players, but he also has to report to the organization's athletic director. The athletic director is responsible for handling all the facilities, uniforms, scheduling, and budgeting for all the sports teams in the organization. He sets guidelines regarding player development, fundraising, and academics. He is responsible for how the athletic organization looks in the media. He also recruits, hires, and fires head coaches.

You may think that the head coaches he recruits are only those with the most wins. Often times that may seem the case, but it isn't the reality. Now this is important, so pay attention. The athletic director defines a successful head coach as one who can keep players returning to the program. Why is this important? The answer is because the parents' and fans' hard-earned money is following the player. This reality is as true in the Olympics, NFL, and World Cup Soccer as it is all the way down to youth leagues all around the world. Money will follow successful programs, and you can't have successful programs without attracting players.

Thus, the athletic director must attract head coaches who attract assistant coaches who attract players. If he does, he and all the coaches can build a successful program, earn good livings, and be pillars of leadership in the community. If he doesn't, players go somewhere else, and coaches get fired and make their spouses upset. They then have to find new jobs and fix their reputations. Are you starting to see how a third party can influence a player-coach relationship?

What's more is that the athletic director reports to another authority figure, usually a president, general manager, or school principal depending on the organization. Youth leagues will have a president. Usually, this is the guy who helped begin the association, raised the initial funds, and made the city contacts to use the field. When the original founder retires, the stadium is named after him and someone else replaces him. In the NFL, NBA, NHL, and MLB, this position is called the general manager.

More than likely a stadium will never be named after a general manager of a professional team, but a good one will select the athletic director who will select the head coach who will have a stadium named after him. Many times in the pros, a general manager and the athletic director are the same person. Either way, you know what the goal is for his responsibilities: to attract money by attracting players.

Finally, a school athletic director reports to his school principal. The school principal is responsible for the success of both academics and athletics. Some school principals care only about one or the other. However, the best ones know that students earn their educations both in the classroom and on the field.

As a player, you should know that there is one more authority figure at the top of your organization. If you are in a youth association, more than likely there is an athletic board which is made up of a group of local parents. These boards can be made up of as few as three to five members, or as many as 20. Often there is a vote among current members to bring in additional or new members. Just know that there is a process for membership in this board. Your association's president reports to this athletic board. Sometimes he is a member of the board and may even be the "chair," or the one who has control over the board meetings. This means that if he has the last word in meetings, he can influence the vote to lean the way he wants it to go. If your association president is the "chair" of the athletic board, he has a lot of power.

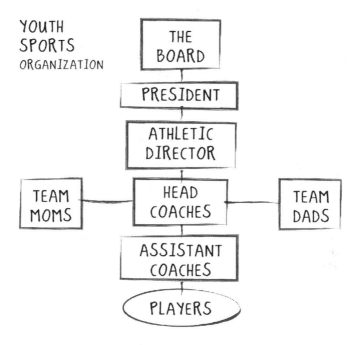

The board's primary job is to select the right association president. How will the board know they selected the right president? You guessed it. They will know it by his ability to attract the right athletic director, who attracts the right coaches, who attracts the right assistant coaches, who attracts players, who bring the parents and fans who give money back to the association.

A school is not very different than a youth association. If you are in a school, your principal has exactly the same responsibility to attract students. You should know that principals attract students to their schools for both athletic and academic reasons. They are judged by a school board, county board, state board, or parent/teacher board made up of elected or appointed individuals. These boards know that money will come back through when they hire successful principals. These board members run the risk of not being re-elected or reappointed to their positions of power if their schools lose students, or they can be re-elected or reappointed to their positions if money flows in regularly. Unfortunately, at these levels many relationships are heavily influenced by third parties, and that means politics. For whatever reason, you as an athlete may not have a choice about which school you will play for, and your school or organization may be suffering from these politics. We'll talk about how this happens and what to do about it later, but for now, just be aware of how the school system operates.

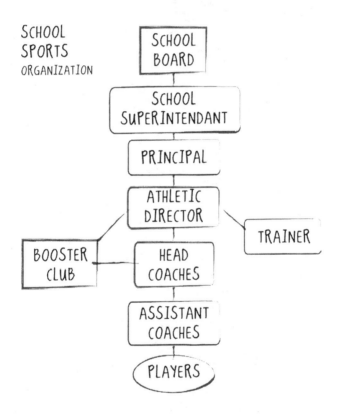

In a professional team, the general manager reports to an owner or owners. The owner of a professional team did one thing to get his title, and that was to write a check for a very large sum of money to buy the team from another owner. Sometimes a group of other owners in the league vote to approve of the sale, but an owner who can write a check rarely gets rejected.

Now, since he wrote a very large check to own the team, how will he determine if he is successful? Right again! He's successful if he attracts the general manager who attracts the athletic director who attracts the head coach who attracts the assistant coaches who attract the players who attract the fans who pay money back to the team which goes to the owner. Sometimes the owner gets his money indirectly by way of fans who buy the products from the advertisers who pay the TV networks who pay the league who pays the owner for the rights to film the game, but either way the owner is successful by way of the players. Are you figuring out how your relationship with your coach can be influenced by third party politics?

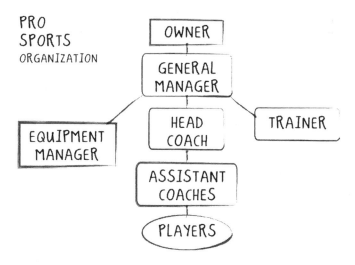

But wait! There's still more. For now, let's just call your youth association, school, or team simply a team. Your team plays in a group against a bunch of other teams, right? Absolutely! Sometimes this group is also called a league, as in the National Football League. Sometimes it's called a conference, such as the Southeastern Conference. Other times it's called an association, such as the National Basketball Association or the National Collegiate Athletic Association. For now, we'll just call it a league. This league is an organization all on its own.

The league has a president who is usually once again chosen by a board of elected or appointed members. The league president has a responsibility to set the rules of the games you play in. He hires officials who abide by those rules. He confirms that players are eligible to play. He judges disputes between teams. He runs a budget to bring attention to the league so he can pay himself and hire those officials. Where does he get that money? Very good! He gets it from the teams who pay to be in the league. How is a league president then successful? Once again, you guessed it! The league president is successful if he can attract the teams who attract the players who attract the fans who pay money back to the teams who pay to play in the league.

Sometimes the same person fulfills many different roles, but I can tell you that every sports organizational structure is basically the same. As an athlete, the sooner you are aware of how this structure works, the sooner you can build a plan to help your athletic career while avoiding those pitfalls that can derail it. Fortunately, there is one very simple way to determine whether or not politics has infiltrated your team or league. It's so easy that a first time T-ball player can determine quickly whether or not his team has been doing the right things.

All you have to do as an athlete is look to the stands and see how many enthusiastic fans are in the seats over several games. If you see a large enthusiastic crowd, the team is doing well, which means that the board/owner approved a good president/principal/general manager, who hired a good athletic director, who hired a good head coach, who hired good assistant coaches, who attracted players. And what follows the players? That's right! Those parents and fans yelling in the seats follow the players, and they write those checks back to the association/school/team!

Of course, populations may vary by region, so some arenas won't be as full as others. If, however, the fans that are there are having a great time, there is a potential that the politics have been minimized and the athletes are having a better time performing for their team. Remember, long athletic careers go to those athletes who consistently put on great performances! Find that organization that will give you the best chance at having a successful career!

# CHAPTER 8

## Knowing Your Coach

**COACH JOE MOORE STOOD THERE** with his pipe, glaring at one of his linemen. The other linemen, standing 6'5" or more, got nervous. One by one they began to shuffle away, leaving the one lineman alone on an island. He looked at his teammates for help, but they gave him a look as if to say, "Sorry, man. You're on your own."

Then Coach Moore removed his pipe, still glaring. The smoke lingered in the air. Finally, it came out. He was disappointed in this player and knew he could be doing better. He let him have it verbally, letting him know all the things the lineman could be doing but wasn't. It was also personal. Coach Moore knew the player had greater potential, and he admonished him for not giving everything he was capable of giving. "The problem is," he said, "you don't think you're a great player deep down inside. If you want to be great, you've got to start with your thoughts! From what I'm seeing, you think you're nothing!"

Eventually, Head Coach Lou Holtz drove over. Knowing the structure, he let his assistant do his thing. However, after five minutes of admonishment and large, grown men feeling nervous, even Coach Holtz felt he had to step in. "Coach Moore," he said. "He's our team captain."

"I don't care if he's our team captain!" Coach Moore responded. "He can't even captain himself!" Coach Moore obviously could not care less about politics and status. He wanted this player to be his best, and being a leader on the team meant that more was expected from him. Coach Moore clearly knew what he was doing, as this player would eventually become an All-American. Coach Moore was a great example of not letting third party influences get in the way of making a player great.

Now that you know how easy it is for third party influences to get in the way of your relationship with your coach, you will want to figure out how much your coach is affected by those politics. There is a simple rating system that you, the athlete, can use to help you determine what kind of coach you have. You'll use two different criteria to determine your relationship with your coach.

The first one is competency. This is pretty simple. Does he know and teach you the ART concept, or does he not? If he can't teach you in terms of the ART concept, he's not competent. If he knows it, but he can't communicate it, he's not a competent coach. It doesn't matter what your coach knows. It matters what you know. Rate your coach in terms of competency, with either a C being competent or an I being incompetent.

The second one is "team focus." This, too, is pretty simple, but you'll have to listen hard to make this determination. However, doing so is critical to knowing what kind of coach you are dealing with. When your coach talks to his players as a group, how often does he use the word "I" versus "we"? I am not talking about times when he says "I" and "you" in the same sentence, such as, "I believe in you," or "I see you making that play." I'm talking about when he says things such as, "I will win a state championship!" or "I am going to beat that other coach!" or "I will have it done this way!" If you hear your coach say these types of sentences referring to himself as "I," rate him an S for being self-focused. If you hear him use "we" when he talks to his players, rate him a T for being team-focused. I'll explain later why this is important.

Now, draw a box with four boxes inside it. At the bottom of the box, write "Competency" and put an I for "incompetent" underneath the left column and a C for "competent" underneath the right column. On the left of the box write "Team" and put an S for "self-focused" to the left of the lower row and a T for "team-focused" to the left of the upper row. Now, grade your coach. It should be a

*CT, CS, IT,* or *IS*. Put an *X* where his score is. We'll talk about what you will likely face when you have a coach in each of these boxes, and what to do about it. During your athletic career, it's very likely that you will experience all four.

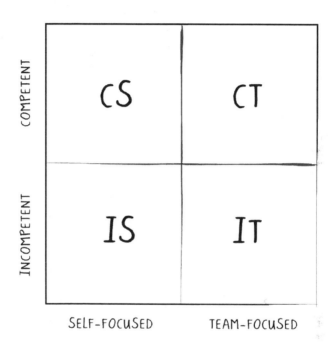

# CHAPTER 9
## A Competent Team-Focused Coach

**OTHER THAN MY FATHER** (and I can't use him as an example because I am biased), one coach who made an immediate impact on me was John Fabris. My sophomore year, John Fabris gave up a prominent coaching position somewhere else to take a pay cut and become a graduate assistant at Notre Dame. He did this just for the experience. As a walk-on linebacker and special teams player, I didn't know how lucky I was that he made this decision.

Coach Fabris began quietly, making sure he had his special teams and defensive scout team depth charts lined up. He didn't coach us much the first few days, other than letting us know that "we" were going to take it to these guys and that "we" had the potential to show the first team how to play football. "We" were just one play away from making it happen. My scout team teammates and I couldn't help but like the guy. "We" enjoyed giving him effort because he was interested in our success.

Then one day he called a meeting for the special teams scout team players only. No first or second string guys were allowed. As players, no one really knew what to expect. "Guys," he said. "I see us out there working hard and giving effort, but we can do better." Coach Fabris then began telling us of his experiences coaching special teams at his prior schools, and how "we" broke all kinds of records at those schools and "we" were ranked up there with the top in the NCAA. I could tell he was very proud of what his former players had accomplished.

"Let me show you how we did it," he continued. "First, when doing a punt return, you have to remember the three Ts, which are 'Tie-up, Trail, and Tag.'" Doesn't it sound like he was telling us certain Rules in the ART concept? If you think so, you're right! It was so simple. No one had taken the time to teach us, and here was this coach telling us how "we" were going to do it.

We were energized going out to practice that day. Coach Fabris, taking that small amount of effort and giving us information that we were hungry for, helped us to have the confidence to play against the first and second string. What's even better is that it worked! The other coaches responsible for the first and second string became irate at their players for giving up touchdown after touchdown to a group of walk-on scout teamers. Those coaches at that time yelled and screamed at them, but they didn't teach them what they were doing wrong. There was no mention of Alignment, Rules, or Technique. There was only "You're not any good!" and "How could you get beat by THOSE guys?!" Obviously, we ran it again, only to have the scout team return two more touchdowns.

John Fabris was promoted to special teams coordinator within two weeks by Head Coach Lou Holtz. Coach Fabris mixed up the personnel, brought up a couple of scout team players, and taught his concept to everyone else. Shortly afterwards we played the University of Texas at Notre Dame Stadium. If memory serves me correctly, Allan Rossum returned two kick returns for touchdowns, and our team jumped inside the top 15 in the country in special teams yardage stats, all because of one game.

I use Coach Fabris as an example because he was a Competent Team-Focused Coach. As far as I am concerned, anyone who hires Coach Fabris or someone like him is making a smart career move because this guy makes and attracts players. You remember what follows players, don't you?

If your coach is a Competent Team-Focused Coach, you probably don't realize how lucky you are. As you listen to him in practice, and you're confident he's a CT, soak up everything you can that he says. Write it down. Remember it. Keep a notebook. This coach is not only teaching you how to be an athlete, he's teaching you how to succeed in life. He'll teach you how to let the game come to you so that you'll be successful. He'll teach you how to direct your effort, and not just give it. He'll teach you how to coach yourself on the field so you can correct your ART on the next play. Be around this coach as much as possible. This coach will make you into a winner!

CT coaches work very well with other CT coaches, and they help bring along Incompetent Team-Focused coaches and some Incompetent Self-Focused coaches. However, it's been my experience that CT coaches are bitter enemies with Competent Self-Focused coaches. Both CTs and CSs are usually at high levels of their profession, but there is a subtle difference you need to know about them that causes this friction. Unfortunately, I believe it's this friction that leaves CT coaches vulnerable to politics if there are some CS coaches higher up in the organization. We'll talk about this as we get further along, but just be aware of what can happen.

# CHAPTER 10
## An Incompetent Team-Focused Coach

**THE SCORE WAS 0-0 UNDER** the Thursday night lights in Las Vegas. Our JV football team was looking for a win against Cimmaron Memorial High School, and defense ruled the day during this particular game. Our defensive coordinator, Coach Yankus, had us all fired up. He was a skinny chain smoker in his early 70s that would tell you that your rear end was grass and he was the lawnmower. We loved playing for him.

Unfortunately, our offense needed help. One after the other the quarters ended in a scoreless tie. The intensity and desperation among our coaching staff could be felt among the players.

Because our offensive coaches didn't understand offensive line blocking, that week they called my father to come help coach the offensive line. He had an immediate impact by showing us the proper Technique, but he also knew it wasn't his place to tell the other coaches what to do, even though their experience paled in comparison to his.

Finally, Dad had to pose a question to the young offensive coordinator. "What's your game plan?"

"What do you mean, 'What's my game plan?'" the young coach shouted back. "We're trying to score a touchdown, Coach!"

In his 6'5" frame, my dad took a deep breath and tried not to lose his cool. "Let me try this again," he said. "What's your game plan?

What do you want me to tell our linemen to do with the plays that you're calling? What plays are you calling to get the defense out of position so that we can score?"

The young coach didn't have an answer. With the play clock ticking, he sent in a play to our quarterback designed to give the tailback the ball down the middle of our formation. Our tailback ran between the center and me and made a great move on the line-backer. As I gave chase, he broke towards the end zone, where he was sandwiched between two defenders. The ball came out and landed in the end zone where I fell on top of it. We still don't really know who scored the touchdown, whether our tailback broke the plan when he was hit or my falling on the ball sealed the deal, but it didn't matter. Our team came away with a hard fought 6-0 victory, even though our offensive coordinator struggled with understanding what a game plan was.

In youth associations, high schools, and many colleges, you'll find a lot of Incompetent Team-Focused coaches, or ITs. When I say "incompetent," I'm not saying that these coaches don't have some knowledge. What I'm saying is that these coaches still have a lot to learn. Often head coaches in youth associations will be ITs. In fact, I would say most of them fit into this category. Even head coaches in high school will qualify as ITs at schools with smaller enrollments. Remember, an athletic director is judged by the ability to attract coaches who attract players, and if he is on a budget, he'll sometimes go with a young head coach that players want to play for rather than a more experienced coach that nobody respects. At the college ranks, your ITs will be assistant coaches. Often they will be graduate assistants. Remember, however, that they are there because they attract players. In college, these guys are given a chance because of their attitude and willingness to learn. Often times, though, they had better prove themselves quickly or else they will quickly be changing professions.

While at Notre Dame, I had a couple of great IT coaches who were just beginning their career. Jay Sawvel came in as a graduate assistant special teams coach after John Fabris left. Because we had things going well, I went up to Jay when I first met him and told him, "I'm glad to meet you. I know you just got here and you're not going to know who the players are. If you'd like, give me a call and I'll let you know who to put where on your special teams depth chart. It might help things go smoothly for you." He thanked me, but I honestly didn't think he'd call.

To my surprise, Coach Sawvel called me while I was in my room one day after class. I knew right then that coach was going to be successful. This guy didn't care about getting credit. He just wanted to get it done. For the next two years, I enjoyed working and dealing with Coach Sawvel. It was no surprise to hear that he found an opportunity to coach under the same head coach for over a decade. His head coach probably knows that Jay Sawvel is able to attract players to his program! In my book, he graduated to a CT very quickly.

Another great IT coach we had at Notre Dame was Justin Hall. Coach Hall had played as an offensive lineman under Lou Holtz and after graduation came back to Notre Dame to begin a career in coaching as a graduate assistant. Being in charge of the defensive scout team, Coach Hall learned quickly that we players pretty much had it under control. However, that didn't mean that he took a break. I remember one practice in particular when I was excited about an upcoming date I had with a girl on campus, and I was obviously not focused on the field. Coach Hall came up to me and said, "So Kunz. What's her name?" I'll never forget that he picked up on that. He was definitely focused on his team and not on himself.

Later in the year, I received a phone call from Coach Hall asking me to come down and see him right away in his office. It was urgent, but he wouldn't tell me what it was about. After class I went to go see him, and he shut the door to a small room and grabbed a marker for the white erase board. "I've got to tell you that you're causing some problems that I have to make you aware of for your own sake," he said.

"Problems!? What problems?" I thought. Quietly I waited to hear what he had to say.

He said, "We had a coaches meeting, and Coach Holtz asked me specifically to list in order the defensive scout team players who have given the most effort." He turned to the white board and began to write down my name and several of my walk-on teammates' names as he went down the list.

Kunz
Burgdorf
Lynch
Grimm
Mulvena
Etc.

"The problem," he continued, "is that there are players that have been recruited and are on scholarship that aren't getting playing time, and they aren't getting playing time because you guys have been giving more effort. This is making some of the other coaches very upset. Because of this, Coach Holtz has declared that these guys are being taken off special teams, but that you guys are getting an opportunity. Congratulations. Just know, though, that some of the other coaches aren't going to like it."

I could only imagine Justin Hall being put on the spot as a first-year graduate assistant in a tense meeting between CT and CS coaches. His answer was going to make enemies either way, but he stuck to his guns about what he believed and chose to make the team better by rewarding effort. Coach Hall, I salute you!

If you decide you have an IT coach, you're going to have to consider it a working partnership. He will know more than you do, but he's not going to know everything. What's important about having an IT coach is that you and he communicate. Remember, you're both in this together. He depends on your success, and you depend on his. Where he'll be able to help you especially is in shielding you from the politics. I found this to be especially true with both Coach Sawvel and Coach Hall. They both wanted me to learn as much of my ART as I could. As we communicated, they were learning how to teach the ART concept so they could develop in their profession. What made these guys special, though, was that they knew they would be successful if the team was successful. Ultimately, these guys both became pros and CT coaches in their profession.

Where ITs run into trouble is how they deal with CS coaches, especially if the CS coaches are in positions of authority. They usually don't have enough experience to argue a case, and they don't agree philo-sophically with the depth chart. Because the value system is different, don't be surprised to see an IT coach look for another job somewhere else as soon as the season is over if he reports to a CS coach.

IT youth head coaches also can have difficulty with CSs. Imagine if one IT youth coach drafts a player who is the son of a former NFL player who is a CS (yes, parents can have rankings, also). Keep in mind that this coach is a guy who doesn't know a whole lot, but believes in certain principles that build a team. Imagine this former NFL player goes to the head coach and says, "You need to put my son at quarterback." Ultimately, this would be a situation where this NFL dad could be right because his son is the best quarterback on the field, or he could be trying to gain preferential treatment for his son. The problem is that the Incompetent Team-Focused youth head coach won't have the competence to know which it is. If he gets this wrong, he could make a mistake, begin to feel self-con-scious, and then fall from an Incompetent Team-Focused coach down to an Incompetent Self-Focused coach as he begins to worry about his own reputation and not the team.

The bottom line is to do all you can to help your IT coach become competent as quickly as he can. Get your teammates and parents to help. Let him know what you see on the field. Let him know what other players think in the locker room. Be a voice for the team. Offer to help when you see an opportunity. You may not be elected captain, but your IT coach is going to need your leadership on the field to help him succeed. Remember, you're both part of the same team, and by working together you'll give yourselves the best chance for success.

# CHAPTER 11
## A Competent Self-Focused Coach

**WE WERE WATCHING FILM** during fall camp, and our coach was teaching all the places our starters needed to be on the field, what they were supposed to do, and how they were supposed to do it. Fellow walk-on Mike Burgdorf and I sat behind the scholarship players taking it all in, though we had a feeling the likelihood of our getting on the field was slim. These coaches wanted to win with their guys, and we weren't a part of their plan.

Suddenly, the coach grew silent and turned off the film. He looked at his scholarship players and said, "Hey, let me ask you guys a question." The players were silent. "If we were playing Southern Cal, and you knew that John Smith was out there at defensive back covering Keyshawn Johnson (USC's best wide receiver at the time), how would you feel?" Obviously, I changed the name of the defensive back. He was a walk-on and a good athlete, but he could be anyone in America. One of the players said, "I'd be scared."

Mike and I looked at each other. We knew that this defensive back was a point of contention in the coaches meetings, but here we were witnessing it first hand, and the coach's question was dividing the team. The player should have said, "Coach, I don't care who you need to play back there. I'm going to give my best for him and the team! And besides, he lines up every day against our best wide receivers, doesn't he? He can take him!"

And the coach, instead of asking the question in the first place, should have asked something to make his players better. For example, he could have asked, "If we need help in this area of our team, how are you going to respond to make the team better?" This coach didn't go that route. He wanted it to be about him and his decisions. This has all the signs of a Self-Focused Coach.

And here's the difference between a Team-Focused Coach and a Self-Focused Coach. First of all, every coach has an ego. Some coaches have greater egos than others, but on a Division I top ten football team, egos are very large. Thus, here's the difference. Team-Focused Coaches are able to place the needs of the team ahead of their own ego. Self-Focused Coaches can't do it. They may struggle with this because of money, fame, or power, but they struggle because of these third party influences.

If we are talking about third party influences, we are talking about— you guessed it—politics. Playing sports taught me more about politics than any of my political science classes I took as an American Studies major. We'll talk more about all the details later, both good and bad, but going through those politics as a player was one of the toughest times I ever had to go through. It also turned out to be one of the best.

If you are a player under a Competent Self-Focused Coach, it's going to be challenging. This is the guy who will say, "I will win a championship!" and "I'm going to do things my way!" in front of team meetings. If his way includes you, congratulations! He may have recruited you and promised you the world. When you begin playing for him, you will notice you will get a lot of attention. He will give you a lot of repetitions while other guys are told to go to the back of the line. These repetitions will quickly make you into a skilled player if you take advantage of it.

But then something happens. Other players will begin to grumble. The coach, in a team meeting, will exclaim, "Only the best athletes will play!" If you're starting, you won't need to worry about what he just said because you're playing. You must be one of the best, right? You might even begin to think that the other guys on the team should just go and join the chess club. Well, you don't mind using them as tackling dummies once in a while.

But then you notice that you don't get many breaks. You've been getting repetitions over and over again, and you keep getting more. He keeps driving you to make you into a great player because he is determined to be a great coach. You are playing all the time, and you never leave the field. Your success is going to prove that he is a great coach. Suddenly, you feel a twinge during a game and have to take a break to see the trainer. Something doesn't work right. You want to play, but your body is tired.

And that's when the surprise hits you. Sure, the backup goes in there, but he hasn't had all the repetitions you have had. Your Competent Self-Focused Coach is now looking disgusted at you for not being on the field. After all, he gave you all those repetitions, and now this is how you repay him, by being injured? This is his team. He's going to do it his way, right? Well, you are his way, now get back in there! But you can't. Maybe he yells at you when the backup makes a mistake. The other team takes advantage of the fact that you are not in there. Now it's your fault for making him look bad.

And that's when the team falls apart. You begin to feel that you were only a means to his end. You never had a real relationship with him. He was only using you to feed his ego, which was being driven by those third party influences. You no longer trust him, and now you have to find another reason to give your effort to the team. Welcome to politics.

On the other end of the spectrum, let's say this Competent Self-Focused Coach's way doesn't include you. Maybe you're an outgoing senior or a walk-on. Maybe you don't fit right in your uniform. Whatever the reason is, this coach has written you off right from the start. He takes one look at you, and your season is already over. You've begun the politics long before the prize recruit.

Surprisingly, I've heard a Competent Self-Focused coach call a senior who has one more year left a "waste" because he hasn't yet broken into the starting lineup. This senior was written off before the season even started, and he didn't even know it.

When players are told to go to the back of the line, one of them will eventually ask the coach what he has to do to get a look. That player will usually get a response about coaches watching film and looking for consistent performance, but it doesn't make sense when that player doesn't even get a chance to be on film to begin with.

Maybe that player will be berated for even asking such a question. I've seen it both ways.

The sad truth is these athletes learn about politics far sooner than the prize recruit. Factions begin to form among the athletes. Some players begin to think that they are more important than the others. Players in the locker room begin to have disagreements. A fight breaks out on the practice field the next day. Coach decides to have a meeting about "not fighting amongst each other," but he doesn't understand that he's the cause of the disunity.

Another coach, usually a CT or an IT assistant, recommends that an undersized player has been working hard in practice and deserves to play. The Self-Focused Coach doesn't like it because it's not his guy. The Self-Focused Coach will even justify his position by asking his recruits how they will feel about the undersized player playing. Of course, the undersized player hasn't had nearly the reps that they have had, so he can't be as good, right? Naturally, they don't like the idea, even though he has played against the starters and performed well every day in practice.

The Competent Self-Focused Coach, influenced by third parties, will establish a culture of politics and poor relationships. As a player, you'll experience frustrations, disunity, divisions, distrust, and depression. You'll get to a point where you'll want to quit. In my time as a player and as a coach, there were five seasons when I had to report to a Competent Self-Focused Head Coach. The first two of those seasons were total disasters. Fortunately, those other three allowed me to discover the only thing that will save a season from a CS Coach, and that is if, and only if, he can be convinced to turn into a Competent Team-Focused coach. It's a painful process, full of risk and frustration. Unfortunately, having gone through it five times, and three of those successfully, I'm convinced it's the only way to save a season and prolong your athletic career.

If you determine you are playing for a CS coach, there are a few things you can do. First, be a Competent Team-Focused player. Remember that it's about the team before it's about any one person. Even if you play an individual sport, you represent everyone who helped you along the way. Those people, whether or not they wear a uniform, are your team. Second, you and your athlete teammates are going to have to do extra work to help the team.

If you are that prize recruit and you have the humility to recognize it, you are going to have to find extra time to help your teammates develop their skills so that they can be ready if anything happens to you. Coach Brian Kelly, an *American Football Monthly* Coach of the Year and the current Notre Dame head football coach, has said in a past issue of American Football Monthly that he has a ranking system for his players. The system is as follows:

1) Can't Play – The player can't be trusted on the field and needs to work on his ART.
2) Can Play – The player can be trusted on the field.
3) All-American – The player is a great contributor as an athlete, but still more is needed.
4) Makes Others Better – You're truly a great player if others are great when they are around you.

If you thought being an All-American was the top rank, you were wrong. The top rank for all of his players is if they have the ability to make others better. Help your teammates learn. The team needs them.

If you are not on your coach's radar, you are going to have to do a few things. First, you too will need to put the team first and be a Competent Team-Focused player. You will have to do everything you are asked, and then you will have to do more. You will have to observe everything that happens on the field and watch everyone's Technique. If you are not paying attention, you won't know what is happening. You will need to understand the ART of your sport in everything you do. Who makes a play and why does he make it? Who misses a play and why does he miss it? Write these things down in a journal so you can remember them.

Then, you will have to use this journal and find time away from practice to develop your own ART abilities. With homework, friends, family, and other activities this can be difficult. However, by just focusing on making sure you understand your Alignment, Rules, and Technique, you can concentrate your efforts in a short amount of time away from practice. Some athletes utilize the help of an outside coach to help with their ART, while others enjoy doing it on their own. Either way, doing this will help you catch up quickly and be ready to make the most of your opportunity when that time comes.

# CHAPTER 12
## An Incompetent Self-Focused Coach

**I CAME TO HELP A FRIEND** of mine coach a youth team at the park. We had just both had a good year coaching at the high school level the previous season, but due to business commitments I couldn't devote the time needed to helping like I could in the past. Still, he asked me to come for a few practices just to get the kids going in the right direction until he found someone else to volunteer.

When I arrived, I was happy to see the players and the potential that they all had. However, something wasn't right. As I came up to my friend, I was surprised by some of the things he was telling me. "I don't have any players," he said. "The organization isn't helping me. They promised me all these things and I'm not getting any of them."

I didn't know what he was talking about. "Isn't this just a game?" I thought. "Don't you see the potential in these kids?" I thought again. As I stood there, the negativity poured from his mouth. I knew right away that these kids were in trouble. This coach couldn't think about the game, and suddenly he was only focused on himself. He would later leave the team with no coach. The organization would scramble to find volunteers to replace him. Fortunately, the volunteers that came in had a great attitude and they were able to have a successful season. However, those players were lucky. Often times when this happens, players have no help when they are facing an Incompetent Self-Focused Coach.

Coaches in this category are typically found at the youth or early high school levels, although they do show up at all levels of play. At the youth levels, an association has too many players and not enough coaches. The athletic director desperately needs to find a coach or else he will have to turn away those players. Why doesn't he want to turn away those players? Very good! Those dollars follow the players!

Looking to get coaches, the athletic director will start asking around if anyone might have any interest in coaching, and he might find a guy who played the sport in high school 10 years ago. Or, a funny example is the father character played by Will Ferrell in the movie *Kicking and Screaming*. The prior coach "cracked under the pressure," so the player's dad, having no athletic experience at all, decided to step up and coach his son's team. Unfortunately, due to a wager between the dad and another coach (the player's grandfather), the dad made it all about him. Thus, the third party influence created the politics that destroyed the relationships and created an Incompetent Self-Focused Coach. It wasn't until the dad realized how the third party influenced him that he moved from being an IS Coach to an IT Coach, leading his team to win the championship game with the help of some Competent Team-Focused Italian players!

The problem with an Incompetent Self-Focused Coach is that there is always a third party influencing him, and playing for him becomes a game of politics. What's worse is that he thinks he already knows everything he needs to know, and he doesn't study the details of the game. His ability to teach the ART concept is very limited. He may know one or even two components of the ART concept, but he will not be able to communicate the third.

He'll often talk about how much he knows, telling war stories of his high school days, but this is only in hopes that he won't be discovered as a fraud. Those third parties that are influencing him can come from many sources. Perhaps he felt slighted by a coach in the past and wants to prove a point. Perhaps a competing coach got under his skin in a parking lot after a game. Perhaps he feels his son is one day going to be a first round draft pick, and he knows if he is the head coach that he can make his son the starting quarterback.

Maybe he doesn't have a very good job or home life, but if he coaches he can be in charge and order other people around. Whatever the reason, this is a very dangerous coach to play for.

Unfortunately, IS coaches also show up in the high school varsity, college, and professional ranks, but as a player you may not recognize these situations until it's almost too late. You may ask, "But aren't coaches at these ranks highly competent in the ART concept?" Usually, yes. However, when that coach is looking for another job while he still has the one he has, he cares less about teaching *you* the ART concept and more about his own situation. Again, he is letting himself be influenced by a third party and politics.

Though there are always exceptions, before coaches change jobs, they more than likely shift from a CT, CS, or IT coach to an IS coach. As a player, you'll suddenly find that you aren't getting the attention you used to get, or that your coach won't come down on you for an ART mistake like he usually does. Then, one day, you'll wake up and hear in the news that your coach just signed a contract with another team. In the sports world, they call this the "coaching carousel." It happens near the end of every season to teams in every sport all around the world.

The sooner you recognize that you are dealing with an IS coach, the better. First, you should always strive to be a CT player, putting the team ahead of yourself and consistently honing your ART skills. However, playing for an IS coach has its challenges. First, if you are playing for a CT coach, you can develop the ART of your sport just by going to practice. If you are playing for an IS coach, however, you are going to have to forget the Techniques your coach teaches you in practice and study on your own the proper Technique. You'll have to hire an outside coach or find some books that can coach you on your ART abilities. Even if you are playing in college and you think your coach may be looking for another job, you'll want to watch film of yourself and find reliable information on your performance because your coach may only tell you what he thinks you want to hear. He knows his relationship with you is going to end, so he will try to soften the blow by playing to your own ego, and that doesn't make you a better athlete. Either way, you'll have to spend additional time and effort learning your ART because you won't be getting the information you need in practice.

As an All-American at Notre Dame, my father learned great blocking Technique. He was such a technician that he was drafted second in the NFL in 1969 to the Atlanta Falcons. Unfortunately, his offensive line coach for the Falcons had a different philosophy for blocking Technique during passing plays. The more my dad studied it, the more he realized that the physics this coach was teaching didn't make sense. Since his coach was an authority figure, he had to humor his coach during practices. When it came to playing actual games, however, he went back to the Technique that made him an All-American at Notre Dame. During his six seasons with the Falcons, he went to the Pro-Bowl five times and was recognized as an "All-Pro" three times. I'd say he made a great decision to look back at the science to make an ART of his game.

That being said, you have to realize that sometimes you are going to be told things that simply don't work. As the science of your game gets more and more advanced, coaches who haven't studied the ART concept in the proper form may tell you to do something that they were told to do in high school, even though it has since been discovered that there is a far better way to do the task. Other times, new Techniques will be tried, but the simple and true stand the test of time. It's your coach's job to know which method to teach. The IT coach will discover that there is a better way and change his teaching methods. The IS coach won't. He will yell at you when you can't do it his way with success. Unfortunately, you'll be frustrated because success won't be and never will be had.

I used to laugh when my dad coached my high school teammates and me while working with an IS coach. This coach would try to argue with my dad about how a Technique should be done or where a player should line up. "So, *how* many times have you been All-Pro?" he'd ask them. The conversation would end every time, and my fellow linemen and I would smile and get back to studying the Techniques my father taught us. It must have worked because four of his linemen went on to play college football. One of us even went all the way, starting at center in the NFL and earning two Super Bowl rings. That's not bad for a small Catholic school with just 27 players on the varsity.

As you are gaining information on your ART, you will also have another challenge under an Incompetent Self-Focused coach, and that's attitude. Your teammates are going to struggle. As player after player begins to discover that your coach is a fraud or is looking for another job, morale is going to suffer big time. Trust among the team will begin to disappear rather quickly. Forget politics. Once they learn the truth about an IS coach, teams and athletes begin to look for survival. Some players quickly decide that they want to move to another team. Some decide to leave the sport altogether. When game day rolls around, you're not looking forward to it because you know you and your teammates are unprepared. Forget winning—you just want to make it out without being on a stretcher.

One of the toughest things you'll go through is learning how to lead when those above you don't know how to lead themselves. It is extremely difficult for a team to have a successful season under an IS head coach. Usually in the first few weeks of the season an Incompetent Self-Focused head coach will be discovered. Also, how many football teams going to bowl games after a great season suffer because they find out their head coach just took a different job?

Again, your best defense is to be a Competent Team-Focused player. During and outside of practice, though, you're going to have to encourage your teammates. Get them to take steps to learn the ART concept away from practice so they can feel more confident during games. Agree that you're not going to play politics and that you'll get through this situation for each other. Play for those who are with you on the field, and not for anyone else. Build those relationships with your teammates. No matter whom you play for, your record depends on you. Focus on ART development and making others better. Then, when the season is over, you can use the experience to prepare your steps next year.

A great example of this comes from the movie *Major League*. When the players and coaches finally realized that they were playing for a conniving Incompetent Self-Motivated owner, they decided the best thing to do was to become Competent Team-Focused athletes and win the championship so she couldn't sell the team and move it to another city. Granted, it seems far-fetched, but you'd be surprised how far politics will go.

# CHAPTER 13
## The Recruiting Process

**IN THE SPORTS WORLD**, everybody gets recruited. True, recruiting may only come through good marketing, but no organization can survive unless good people are attracted to be a part of it. We already went through the organizational process that describes how, at the youth level for example, associations are recruited by leagues, and board members are recruited by associations. Presidents are recruited by the board. Athletic directors are recruited by the president. Head coaches are recruited by the athletic director. Assistant coaches are recruited by the head coach. Finally, players are recruited by the coaches, and the parents, fans, and money follow the players. Yes, certain rules may prohibit an athlete or an athlete's parents from talking with a coach directly, but if you can read and see the excitement in a program, you're being recruited by marketing. Good marketing is good recruiting.

As an athlete you first need to know what your options are. For example, is there more than one league for you to play in? Maybe some leagues have rules that better fit your situation. Maybe others are closer. Maybe you want to get to the very top league in your sport. Which league of your choice sends the most athletes to the next level? You'll want to decide.

Second, once you select a league, is there an association or school you want to play in? When you go to a game, which one has a large, vibrant crowd? Maybe cost is a factor, or proximity to your home is more important. Here's a thought. Which association or school places an emphasis on teaching the ART concept and character development? How do they emphasize this? Take some time thinking about these issues, because after this, you won't have many other options.

Once you sign the forms and your family writes a check to play for a school or an association, you essentially belong to them. If you earn a scholarship at a college or get drafted in your professional league, you belong to them. If they didn't tell you the truth and you fell for it, you'll find out very quickly. Remember that they succeeded in attracting a player (you) and getting money to follow the player (either by way of your check or by excited fans buying your jersey along with ticket sales). Once you belong to them, you will eventually discover that you don't have a choice as to which coach you play for.

Let's say you've just been drafted in the NBA, for example. You're excited that you have a great head coach who you feel will take you to the championship. A month after being drafted, however, your head coach is offered a job for a ton of money to another team. He leaves and takes all of his qualified assistant coaches with him. Can you suddenly stand up and say, "Hey, I'm coming with you!" Unfortunately, you belong to the organization, not the coach. Until the terms of your contract are up, you're not going anywhere.

Colleges and high schools operate much the same way, except that they do have clauses that allow athletes to change schools due to hardship. However, often league rules stipulate that the athlete must not play a full season if he does make a change. This isn't always the case, but it should be noted. Sometimes in college, if a player wishes to transfer to a different school, a coach will sign papers granting a release, but only if the player has proof that he is not going to transfer to certain schools that will play his future former team.

In the youth organizations, it's very likely that you will have a week of "evaluations." This is a week where all the coaches will watch you and every other player perform drills and show your abilities. Organizations do this to help their coaches see the players so that they can make their selections during a draft. Strong organizations like to have evaluations for the sake of attracting quality head coaches. Head coaches like to win, and if they can't see what players they are drafting, how can they know they have a chance to win? Thus, the weekend after evaluations, all the coaches get together and hold a draft.

If a coach drafts you, you will have to play for him whether or not you like him. It's either that, or your parents ask for a refund minus the deposit and they write another check for you to play for another league. This costs your family more money. When you go to the other league, you again won't have a choice as to which coach you will play for. Are you seeing how this works? This is why it is so important to determine which organization you want to play for ahead of time. Do your homework.

One year, I was coaching a Division II team made up of 10- and 11-year-olds with some friends of mine. The Division I team was made up of athletes selected by the Division I head coach. They would play the top talent from association teams all around the city. If a player was not selected by the Division I head coach, he fell into a pool of kids that would play a Division II schedule. These Division II kids didn't play all around the city, but they played in games against each other in our own park. We had our own schedule, our own playoffs, and our own trophies. Division II was less hassle, just as competitive, and a lot of fun.

That year, the Division I coach made his team selections, and one quality athlete surprisingly wasn't among them. We felt this athlete had some potential to be our starting running back, so we drafted him in the first round. As we went through the draft, I felt we had a great Division II team.

However, the next day I received a phone call. Apparently, our first-round running back draft pick was upset that he was not selected to play on the Division I team. I heard that his parents were even more upset. Rather than finding out what kind of coaches drafted him and how much experience we had to offer, they decided to pull out of our association in protest and join the high school feeder team. The excuse his parents gave was that they wanted to improve his chances for his "high school career." He was 11. He went to the feeder team, fell to last on the depth chart, and didn't play. The feeder system was sure glad to take their money, though.

On the other end of the spectrum, we had drafted another kid to carry the ball that same year. This kid played Division II and had a great time. We had a great season and lost a tough game in the play-offs. He became a real leader. Though he could have gone to play in the high school feeder system the next few seasons, he had fun in our organization and kept coming back. When he finally did go to high school, he found a home at outside linebacker and started for a state championship team. The Division II kid had a far better high school career. He was prepared because he found quality coaching in his youth league and because his organization attracted quality coaches. He had fun! On the other hand, I'm not sure if our first-round draft pick ever played again.

Out of high school, my own recruiting experience was somewhat of a disaster, but it worked out in the end. Looking back, I recognize that I really didn't have a plan. Starting in my sophomore year, some of my teammates and I received our first recruiting letter from Akron University. Our head coach had some connections throughout the country, and one of his connections was starting early to develop a relationship. Still, I never forgot that feeling of getting that first letter.

As our junior year approached, different letters came to us. We received letters from Ivy League schools, smaller Division I-AA, II and III schools, and even a large Division I-A school every now and again. Our coach's connections seemed to be helping us gain interest.

And then it happened. Our coach was let go due to some reckless behavior that damaged school property. He was asked to resign right before classes ended for the summer. Once he left, all those connections left with him. The athletic director asked if a psychology teacher, who was looking ahead to retirement, would step up on late notice and captain the ship of our team. Heading into our senior year, the year we needed to show what we could do to earn our scholarships, we had several changes to deal with. The way it all happened left us searching for answers.

As we played our season, we were not better than average. If college coaches ever watched us, it's because they came to scout the talent on the other team. There was was no Internet in those days, so if you wanted to get noticed, you had to have film made of your games, cut a highlight of that film, and send it to colleges. Hopefully you'd get a call back. Our prior coach was efficient at using game film for the benefit of his players. Unfortunately, this technology was beyond our nearly retired coach, so we didn't get copies of game film for our own use. In order to have something made, our parents bought camcorders and had them pointed at us during the games. In the recruiting world, we were definitely lacking.

As our season ended, I made up my highlight tape and sent it on to a few colleges. There were no return calls. Nobody wanted to look at a 6'0 tall 210-pound offensive guard/defensive tackle. Then suddenly, I received a phone call in January from some coaches from the University of Montana. They were coming down to see one of our other linemen, and thought they'd stop by. I was in the middle of my wrestling season, and I had dropped weight down to 195. Knowing this, I thought that they'd look past my current weight and we'd discuss Technique, position changes, etc. Not even two minutes into the meeting, I could tell that they were not going to offer anything. They were there because they heard my father was an eight-time Pro Bowl NFL lineman and had an undersized son. They didn't know I'd be only 6'0" and 195. As they left, they said that they'd send some material to me. I knew as they left that I would never hear from them again. Still, I thought it was cool to be visited by some college coaches.

Signing date came and went. Grey, our center, was successful in signing a scholarship to Arizona State. Another player signed to play for UNLV. Realizing I had to do something, I filled out college applications the traditional way and began sending them out. I hate to say it, but letting myself be unprepared prior to my senior season caused me to scramble when everything ended. I just didn't antici-pate something happening with our head coach. Once my wrestling season ended, I went back to lifting weights, gaining weight, and filling out applications. Even as the weeks passed, I still knew I was going to play for someone. I just didn't know who that would be.

Then one day I got a call. It was from Nick Holt, who was then coaching with John L. Smith at the University of Idaho. Nick had coached at UNLV, and he was asking his former colleagues about players on the West Coast that may have been overlooked after signing day. One of the coaches at UNLV had mentioned my name. They had forwarded my game film to him, and he gave me a call.

"Matt, I took a look at your game film, and you're a good football player," he said. You know what, it may be a line he told all his recruits, but it was great to hear it after all I was going through. "We'd like to invite you on up to our school, take a look around, watch practice, and see if you'd like to join the Vandals."

I was honored and excited. The Vandals at that time were a very competitive team in Division I-AA, having gone far in their playoffs each and every year. It was also a good engineering school, and at the time I thought I would like taking classes in engineering. They also had a good reputation for hiring good coaches. Usually, their coach was hired to go to a larger school, and the next one was later hired to go to a larger school, as was the next one after that. The administration knew how to attract good coaches.

Still, seeing as how I had all these other college applications out there, we had already planned a college trip to see some of the ones I was more interested in. While my mother and I were on this trip, my dad called to let me know that I had received something in the mail from Notre Dame. Dad opened it, and it said that they had received my application, that I was not accepted, but that they had me on their waiting list.

Now, I wasn't really excited about Notre Dame because I had been compared to my father all my life. There was a time when I thought I was going to be 6'5" just like him. I can't count how many of my father's friends would bend down to me and ask if I had plans to be a big-time football player at Notre Dame or in the NFL. I heard it at least once every two months since the time I was able to remember. Obviously, when I stopped growing as a freshman in high school, I had to come to grips that God had other plans for me. Still, I knew Notre Dame was a good school. I liked to watch their games, and I wore the ND hat. I even took a date to go see the movie *Rudy*, which had just come out that year. Would I ever go to Notre Dame, though? I didn't think it was in the cards for me, just because I figured I had to be different.

At one point that January as I was filling out college applications, I took a test to determine which school in the United States would best fit my personality. My grandfather recommended it, so I was not sure if it would help. A month later, I received results in the form of a ranking list. Number "1" at the top was Notre Dame. I basically shook my head, crumpled up the results, and threw them away. "That was a waste of time," I said. Still, I thought I'd go ahead and write an application to Notre Dame out of respect for my grandfather.

When I heard I was on Notre Dame's waiting list, I thought to myself, "I have a 3.7 GPA, and I'm taking all honors courses. I am a captain of two varsity sports. I'm an Eagle Scout and a part of the National Honor Society. What else do they want?" One of the schools I was considering was the Air Force Academy, who often played football against the Irish. I was half-tempted to go there to play against Notre Dame just because of that letter.

Finally, Dad made the suggestion when we came back from our trip that we should "just go look at Notre Dame, just in case." Even though I was angry at Notre Dame and had no intention of going there, since he made the offer, I agreed—but only on the condition that we went during school days so I could get out of classes.

I remember flying into Chicago O'Hare airport on an April Monday and then making the late night drive into South Bend. I had fallen asleep in the car, but I vaguely remember my eyes opening up in time to see the Golden Dome across the hazy black sky above Notre Dame. As we made the turn down Notre Dame Avenue, my dad, excited to be back to his alma mater, shook me on my shoulder and said, "Matt, wake up! There's the Dome!"

I quietly said, "That's nice," and rolled back to sleep.

"Well! If you don't want to see it, we can just turn around and head back home!" Dad said. I knew that wasn't going to happen, so I didn't answer. We rolled up into the circle drive of the Morris Inn, and I remember seeing the ND emblem etched into the hallway carpet and thinking how cool it was as we made our way towards our room.

The next day, we walked around campus. We met with some of my father's former coaches, George Kelly and Roger Valdeseri, who were at that time helping out in the athletic department as they neared retirement. They talked about walking onto the football program as a non-scholarship player. They asked about my speed. They were very happy to have breakfast with us, but I could tell they were most happy to see my dad again after so many years. Still, they arranged a meeting for us to meet Coach Lou Holtz in his office for a few minutes. They also mentioned that the football team was having their scheduled private scrimmage in the stadium that afternoon, and that we were welcome to come and watch.

After a meeting with an engineering professor, my dad and I hit the bookstore and then made our way to meet Lou Holtz. I admit that it was interesting seeing in person the man that I had watched on TV so many times. Dad did most of the talking, mentioning that we were inquiring about my walking on the team, and asking what Coach Holtz's thoughts were about walk-ons. "We have some good ones," he said, "but we only need those who are willing to do the work." He also invited us to the team scrimmage, and shortly thereafter, my dad and I made our walk into the House That Rockne Built across the street.

As we entered the stadium, I had to admit that it was something else. Still, it was for somebody else, not for someone who obviously wasn't going to grow to be 6'5" like my father. I looked at the old bleachers and thought of how this was the same field my dad played on when he was my age. I looked over to watch the offensive lineman, and I realized I had to forget 6'5". These guys were all a full 6'8" across the board. They were pure giants.

As my dad talked with old acquaintances, I left to go to the other side of the field. A young man drove by me on a golf cart, and I could tell something was different about him. I would later find out that his name was "Keith" and that he had some physical and speech challenges, but I could tell he enjoyed being around the players. His golf cart had stickers all over it labeled "Notre Dame's #1 Fan" and "Go Irish!" If he pressed a button in front of him the "Notre Dame Fight Song" would play. I thought it was great that the team took an interest in him and allowed him to come to practices.

As I made my way to the other side of the field to watch the first play of the scrimmage, I came to a player wearing a cast who had been given the responsibility of holding the chains. He looked at me and said, "So why are you here?"

"I'm in high school and thinking of walking-on here." I said.

I was still regaining my weight from the wrestling season. He looked me up and down and said, "So, what are you? A kicker?"

I had to laugh. That's probably what those Montana coaches thought when they left my house a few months earlier. I didn't answer. A second later, the offense lined up and ran an isolation play against the first team defense. As the pads of the fullback and the inside linebacker met, the crack echoed across the empty stadium. I admit it was an incredibly violent display. The speed, size, and strength of these players were far greater than anything I had seen in high school. I loved it.

As play after play unfolded, something suddenly told me, "You know, Matt. You can play with these guys." I don't know where the thought came from, though after many of my other experiences, I wonder if it didn't come from God. It was the first time I can remember that a thought that ran counter to everything came suddenly into the depths of my being. Someone was working on me, but I was still angry. After all, Notre Dame didn't want me. However, it felt like someone wanted me to want Notre Dame. Though on the outside I stood there being calm, on the inside I wrestled with whoever that was.

As the scrimmage ended, my dad and I left to go eat, and I felt victorious over that inner voice. Over dinner, my dad was very excited. "What do you think?" he asked, but I couldn't say that I wanted to go to Notre Dame.

"It's okay," I said. "I'm sure it was great for you, but I don't think it's for me." Feeling dejected, my dad and I had the rest of our meal in silence. I'm sure he thought I was going to ruin my life.

That was when I got up to use the restroom. As I exited the restroom, in front of me was Keith sitting in his wheelchair. Immediately, I recognized him as the same man who was in the golf cart at the stadium. As I tried to get around him, he stopped me and asked with some effort, "Hey, are you a student at Notre Dame?"

Politely I responded, "No. I'm in high school and trying to figure out where I should go."

That's when he looked me in the eye and said, "Well, it's a good place."

After a pause, I said, "Okay. Tell me why."

Then, sitting in his wheelchair, he said to me, "It's a place where people will really take you for who you are." What he was saying was the people at Notre Dame recognized him for what he knew he was, not just what other people thought he was from his outward appearances. What he said got to me, and after I said "thank you" to my new friend, I sat back down in front of my dad like I had just been hit by a ton of bricks.

We drove back to the Morris Inn in silence, and when we arrived, I told my dad that I was just going to walk the campus by myself. That evening, I remember getting lost, going by the Basilica and around the Dome. In the distance, I heard the energy coming from the students who were watching the Bookstore Basketball Final Four, though at the time I didn't know what the noise was. I could feel this place calling me, I thought. From the trees, to the sky, to the lights, to the old buildings, I was beginning to feel at home.

I was a fool for being angry, and for being disappointed that I was not the star athlete so many people expected me to be. Up to this point in my life, I knew that I had accomplished what I had accomplished because those things were worth fighting for. All of a sudden, God had wiped away my anger and my disappointment. Then, he had opened my eyes to show me a place worth fighting for. As I walked around the Notre Dame campus that cool April Tuesday, I realized that I didn't want to leave tomorrow. I didn't want to leave at all. I started to realize that I was feeling more at home at Notre Dame than I ever did at my own home in Las Vegas. For some reason, by the grace of God, I belonged here. The next day, as my dad and I flew out of Chicago to head back west, I looked out the window over the horizon at sunset. I said to myself, "If I get accepted to Notre Dame, I'm going. No matter what, I'm going."

The following week, my dad and I took our trip to Idaho. I had a great time watching the Vandals football team scrimmage in front of the Kibbie Dome, and I enjoyed the tour of the campus. As much as I liked the coaches, the engineering program, and the atmosphere, it wasn't Notre Dame. I knew that I wanted to fight for Notre Dame, and all I needed to do was to get accepted.

Weeks later, I received a call from Coach Holt. It was time to put up or shut up. They wanted me, but if I didn't accept their offer to come to Idaho right then, they were going to give it to someone else. I told him that I was still waiting to hear from Notre Dame, and I hadn't yet heard from them. When I hung up the phone, I had no more scholarships, and all my chips were on the table betting on Notre Dame.

The next day, I received a call from the Las Vegas Notre Dame Club president saying that the University of Notre Dame acceptance committee was in a room, right then, and that they needed me to fax them a list of every single one of my accomplishments. I had just received the "Most Outstanding Senior Young Man" award for my high school, and they wanted me to take a picture of it and fax the picture right there and then. They wanted references written on my behalf right then. They wanted this and that, and it all had to be in the next 15 minutes.

Panicked, I drove all over town trying to get this done, but it just couldn't be done in the time allotted. After 45 minutes of going crazy, I looked up at the sky and thought of God. Is this really what He wanted me to do? After I got home, I went to bed frazzled. I felt I had left all those who were fighting for me down because I couldn't do the impossible. Also, I had no idea what the future would be. I just told the one school who wanted me to play football that I wasn't as interested in them as I was in someone else. I knew that their offer had already gone to some other athlete.

By late June, I was still holding out. The pressure was great. People would ask, "So, what's your backup plan?" Truth be known, I didn't really have one. One night, I kneeled down next to my bed and prayed, "Okay God. You've seen all the things that have been going on with my college selection. You've seen how crazy it has been for me. You also know that I want to go to Notre Dame. I want to fight for that school and for the principles it stands for. However, I also know that You are God and that You have a plan for me. I would really like it if You would make it so that I go there. However, whatever Your will is for my life over the next four years, I will accept that because I know that You know what's best for me. Amen." Afterwards, I lay in bed awake and at peace, thinking of a future controlled by God.

Over the course of my life, it has always surprised me how quickly God can answer prayer. The very next day, while I was at work, I received a phone call from my parents. They had just received a call from Notre Dame, and I had been accepted by the committee. While everyone was congratulating me at work, I couldn't help but think of my prayer to God the night before. He wanted me to know that His will was for me to go there. What's more, He wanted me to trust Him with His will.

As much as God wants to see His children grow in His plan for them, He desires first that we trust Him and have a relationship with Him. That's what He wanted from me before He let His plan take effect. During that night of prayer, after all the confusion, pressure, and waiting, I finally got to the point where I made the choice that I would fight for whatever God wanted me to fight for, and that He would show me what that was. He wanted me to fight for Him, not just Notre Dame. Understanding this would prepare me for the battles I would face over the next four years, as well as the battles I would face over the course of my life.

\* \* \*

Many years later, I had a young man come up to me to ask me about being recruited. He was a wide lineman. Though just over 6'1", I could tell he was very strong and would be looked at near the end of the season. His dad told me that two Division I schools were looking at him, but they were upset that more schools weren't banging down his door.

"Do you like the teams that are talking with you?" I asked him. He said that he did, but he wanted to talk with more teams. "Why?" I asked him. He and his dad stared at me blankly, as if I should know that everyone wants to talk with as many teams as possible. After all, isn't that what you're supposed to want as an athlete? I already figured that this is what they were being sold by all the college recruiting services around today.

"Okay," I said. "Suppose that you have 80 teams knocking at your door. What does that do for you? After all, you can only choose one, can't you?" They nodded in agreement. I continued, "And what good does it do you if you don't like any of those 80 teams?" They looked at each other like I was crazy. Surely they would like one of those 80 teams, wouldn't they?

"You see," I said, "wanting to get a large number of schools banging down your door during recruiting season only feeds your own ego. There's no purpose to that, and there's no relationship that exists. Plus, it's one-sided. You're putting yourself out there like some horse up for auction, only going to the highest bidder. Rather than building a relationship with a team you want to fight for, you're letting your decision be influenced by a third party."

The dad saw where I was going. He admitted that the athlete's mother was the one who was upset that more schools were not looking at her son. However, with the whole family being new to the process, they didn't know how they needed to proceed. Thus, they fell in line with the ego-driven political system that puts third party influences in the middle of the athlete's decision. I wasn't surprised when I heard this, as many well-meaning mothers and fathers will do anything in their power to help their child. Still, it's wrong.

"You've got to understand," I said, "that playing sports for a team is not an easy thing to do. As you advance each level, the competition gets more and more difficult. You sacrifice your time, your family, your friends, your body, and your experiences for the sake of an organization that may or may not care to remember you when you're gone. As much as there will be good times, there will be many times when you will be asking yourself whether or not it's all worth it. When you get up at five a.m. after four hours of sleep to go work out while your roommates get to sleep in, you'll know what I'm talking about. Also, what if you get injured and can't play at the level you used to? What then?"

"Here's the thing," I continued. "You're a unique individual with a lot to offer as an athlete, and you're looking for a relationship with a team that you will be willing to fight for even when it gets very hard to do so. It doesn't do you any good to get a scholarship to a team that you don't want to play for, does it?" He and his dad both agreed. "What you need to do during the next year is focus on building relationships with organizations that you want to play for. If you don't have a list of 10 or 20 programs to choose from, then you don't know what you want. You'll need to first write a list of all the experiences you'll want to have over the next four years, and then start looking at organizations that will fulfill those experiences. Prioritize the importance of those experiences, and use that as a tool to help prioritize the organizations in which you have an interest." They agreed that they could do that.

"After you do that, you'll have to put your ego aside," I said. "You'll have to call the organizations that you are interested in, tell them that you are an athlete, and that you are seriously considering competing for an organization like theirs. If you are talking with a coach, they will ask you all sorts of questions like height and weight, speed times, GPA, and if you have any film. No matter what you tell him, it's important to know that he is not going to believe anything you say. He is only going to want to see the film so he can make his own determinations. This is not necessarily a bad thing, but it is the truth."

I continued, "If all goes well and you're the best athlete the world has ever seen, you'll get a call from the head coach saying that he's coming to town to see you tomorrow with some papers for you so you can sign your life to him for the next four years. However, you know as well as I do that the odds of this happening aren't all that common. If you were the best athlete the world has ever seen, you wouldn't have had to make that phone call. You would have already been discovered. What will happen, more than likely, is that he'll tell you he saw your film and that the coaching staff appreciates your interest. He won't tell you anything else."

"He does this for a reason," I said. "The coach knows that he'll have a certain number of spots for his team. He needs to attract those players who will attract fans, which brings in money for the organization. Thus, the first athletes the coach is looking for are the best of the best. He is going to leave as many spots open as possible so that he can fill his team with these players. This goes for the big name programs all the way down to Division III. Fortunately for you, the coach knows that he has to have some backup athletes he can call upon to fill those spots he has left when all the best athletes are committed. That's where you come in."

"During the season, while you're not getting those calls," I continued, "hopefully you kept calling those 10 or 20 programs on your list. You sent all of those coaches updated film, a couple of letters letting them know how your last game has gone, and maybe even set a date to visit. You asked your current head coach to write a letter on your behalf to the coaches at these programs, explaining how great of a leader you are to have on the team. Your current head coach should want you to find a home in college because he can use your story to attract more quality kids to his own program and bring in the money to keep his job."

Before we parted, I let the athlete and his father know that it's alright to manage your own list of organizations. If you don't decide what you want, you'll be pulled in many different directions without an aim. What's worse, you might run the risk of making a decision that you'll regret. Develop those relationships with those programs that exemplify your values. Know ahead of time what you want to get out of the experience while playing for them, and let your wishes be known. If they don't agree with your values, you'll want to cross that organization off your list and go to the next.

When it comes to making an agreement to play for an organization, such as a college scholarship, be aware that you are then letting your decision be influenced by a third party. If you decide to make an agreement but you don't yet have the relationship with the organization, you are making a very risky decision. You may find that you made a poor choice, and you won't want to play to your potential. It'll be an effort to give your best to a poor program. You will not want that.

Before you decide to make an agreement, be sure to understand the values of the organization that is making the offer. Who is the coach you'll be working with each day? Is he Team-Focused and Competent? How about the athletic director? Ask yourself the same question. Does the program attract other talent similar to or better than you? Do their games bring in spectators? Will they have a plan for you in the event of an injury? Will playing for this organization help prepare you for life not only in the next season, but for the next 40 years of your life? These questions and others are the questions you'll want to ask before signing and making an agreement to play.

Finally, when you go through the decision process and you do choose an organization, you are now committed. You have chosen to represent yourself, your parents, and your teammates on the field of battle. There will be no more hiding. Everything you do from this point on will show the world who you are. Will you give your best effort each day in practice? If not, it will show on the field. Are you a good sportsman? If you are, people will see it, and you may give yourself future opportunities. I have always told my players that sports don't just build character, they reveal it. Once you make the decision to play for a team, you need to now focus all your efforts on being the best athlete that you can be.

There is one more thought you should know. Some organizations are capable of change. To illustrate this point, my father was once asked to come to speak to a youth football organization outside of

Atlanta, GA, while he was playing for the NFL's Atlanta Falcons. They invited him to come and watch practice before they gathered everyone around to hear my father speak. As the teams practiced, my father was shocked at the violence the coaches preached to the athletes. They taught no Technique, and only emphasized reckless-ness with no regard for player safety. These coaches were definitely Self-Focused and Incompetent.

When practice was over, they gathered the players and coaches to listen to my dad. To their surprise, my dad called out the athletic director and told him that he should be embarrassed to allow an organization to be run like this. Dad said in front of everybody that sports are not about glorifying violence but about teaching life les-sons. Dad also told him that they should be ashamed that they did not emphasize player safety. Their athletes deserved better.

The athletic director, obviously upset, stood up and said, "How dare you tell us how to run our organization!" Dad had said the right thing, but they didn't want to hear it. He left without a thank you or applause. As the years went on, Dad would always talk with sadness as he retold this event in his life. He felt sadness years later that a group of adults would preach violence as they had, and he felt that there was no way they would ever decide to change the program after the way the athletic director responded to him. This experience was also why my father wouldn't allow me to play youth football with my friends prior to high school.

Thirty years later, I attended a speech given by former NFL defen-sive lineman Joe Erhman. Joe was written about in a book called *Season of Life*, which talked about how he had given his life to Christ after a wild stint in the NFL. He realized that he had been taught violence as a young man, and anger propelled his athletic career. Later, he realized his need to forgive and decided that there had to be a different way. He began coaching a high school team out of Maryland that emphasized every player playing, and every player having value no matter the situation. They built a culture of love among the players, each building the other up. The result of this was a team that was consistently ranked in the *USA Today* national polls. The story in *Season of Life* was sent to programs all around the country, and Joe was often asked to speak about his philosophy to organizations. I had read the book as a coach, but I also went for another reason. Joe Erhman was one of my dad's teammates with the Baltimore Colts. They had practiced against each other for many seasons in the NFL.

Before Joe's speech, I went up to introduce myself as the son of George Kunz. He just grinned when he heard this. The bond of teammates can run very deep, and I could tell that he was glad I came to say hello.

When Joe began speaking, one of the first things he did was introduce me to the audience. I was surprised he did this. He began to talk about my father and how great of a player he was, and how it's a shame he was not in the Hall of Fame. Then he began to discuss his coaching philosophy.

After he was done and the crowd gave him his applause, I stood up to work my way out of the room. Before I could, though, a silver-haired man in his 60s walked up to me and asked if I was really George Kunz's son. I said I was, and he looked at me and said, "I have to tell you many years ago I was a part of a youth football organization. At one point, we invited your father to come and speak. We were very happy that he was willing to come, but when he saw what we were doing, he admonished us for the way we were coaching our athletes. We didn't like to hear what he said at all. In fact, we were downright angry. However, we held several meetings after that event and realized that he was right. We made several changes to our organization in the way we taught our coaches and the way we coached our players. If your dad hadn't said what he had said to us that day, we would have wound up hurting more players than we ever could have helped. So please tell your father that, after 30 years, he made a difference, and tell him I said 'thank you.'" Through courage, this organization had been able to change, and those changes helped benefit thousands of athletes over the years and will continue to do so now and in the future.

Finding a team to play for requires due diligence. Doing your homework won't prevent every bad situation, but it will definitely increase your odds of having a good experience. More than anything, though, you'll want to find a team that you want to play for. Define what exactly it is you want, and before you sign on the dotted line and someone writes a check, make sure that you've covered your bases so that you'll be inspired to give your team your best!

# CHAPTER 14
## Building Your Personal Team

I ONCE COACHED A YOUNG ATHLETE, about nine years old, who was offered private lessons with me by his parents. On several occasions, the athlete would come to practice and just go through the motions, never giving me his best. On one particular day, this young athlete seemed to forget everything we had gone over in previous lessons.

"That's it. We're done," I said. "You're not coming back to see me until you have paid your dad back for this lesson."

The kid's eyes opened wide and said, "What? I'm only nine years old. How am I going to pay him back?"

I said, "That's not my problem. That's between you and your dad. You will have to work it off somehow. I don't care how, but until he says you have worked it off, you're going to have to find some other way to learn to compete on the field."

The kid complained to his dad, but his dad just smiled and said, "I guess we had better find a way for you to work it off."

"Don't make it easy on him," I said. "He needs to know the value of what you're doing for him." We parted ways, and I received a call from the athlete's father a week later. His son had worked it off through raking leaves, knocking down spider webs, taking out the trash, cleaning dishes, making his bed, and washing the dog. When they came back to see me, the athlete was 100% focused. No longer was he going to take advantage of his team, but he was going to appreciate what they were doing for him.

As an athlete, you are an individual. Even if you are on a team sport, you are still one piece of the overall puzzle for your team's success. However, life constantly throws challenges your way. Unless you recognize that you cannot do it alone, you will struggle handling all the demands that go with playing your sport and managing those life challenges. You will need others to help you focus your skill development in the ART concept and to help you manage your time.

For example, let's say you are a college athlete. You'll need someone to help train you in the ART concept. This role is usually played by your position coach, though you may hire others to help you develop your skill set. Some other coaches you hire could be skill specific. For example, you might have one coach to help you specifically with speed training, another coach to help you specifically with strength training, and a third coach to help you specifically with position drills. There are numerous examples of coaches to help you be a better athlete.

However, you also need help managing situations off the field. When I'm referring to building your personal team, I mean that you'll need people to fill important roles to help you with those things off the field so you can spend more time developing your skills, watching film, and focusing on your ART. If you are that college athlete, you will need someone to fulfill the role of trainer to help with injuries. You will need a class counselor to be available to help you earn your degree. You might need a tutor to help you with a specific class. You will need a mentor to help you understand the social impact of being an athlete. You will want an "advisory council" to answer your questions when important situations come up.

For example, I've heard of one college athlete who had a chance to go to the NFL. He knew that situations would come up that might put him at risk, so he made an offer to a friend of his who happened to be a finance major. The offer was this: If the friend would keep the athlete out of trouble, after the draft the friend would manage the athlete's money and get paid to do so. It all worked out for both of them. Still, I often think more heads are better than one, so I think the athlete would have served himself more if he had added more than one person to his advisory council.

There are other questions you'll need to ask as you think of roles: Who will help you with your travel to and from practice? How might you be able to develop your skills further away from practice, and who can help you with that? Who is going to help you with your diet? Who will help you manage your finances so you can afford to play? Where might you go to study your sport, either via film or through literature, and who can help you with your technology? Who can you go to at church to help you keep life as an athlete in perspective? Who can you go to for advice on relationship issues? Who will help you with equipment? Who can help you find a good organization to play for? Who could help you pick a sports agent? Who could you call on to help you with maintaining your home? Who can help you plan your athletic career?

Although the same person can play different roles, it's important for you to know which people play which roles. You'll want to have each of these people on your phone's speed dial and saved into your contacts. If you successfully recruit the right people to help you, they will gladly offer their help to make sure they get to watch you play. However, there will be more. You'll need to communicate why you are recruiting them to help you. You'll also need to communicate to them how they can best help you. Which role do you need them to fill? What exactly will they need to do in that role? Finally, you'll need to answer the question, "What's in it for them?" If they don't have a reason to help, they may one day bail on you when you need them most, and you'll have to spend time recruiting someone else to fill that role. On the other hand, if their motivation is immoral, they can get you in a lot of trouble and ultimately ruin your career.

Take Michael Vick, for example. Coming into the NFL as a tremendous athlete, Vick kept in close contact with friends from his neighborhood. Without formally announcing it, Vick allowed these friends to form his advisory council, giving him instruction on how to spend his money and his time. Unfortunately, these friends led Vick down a path that involved some terrible crimes, which ultimately caused him to have to go to jail. While Vick was in jail, he found himself facing bankruptcy as his NFL career flew out the window.

Fortunately for Vick, former Head Coach Tony Dungy reached out to him. Coach Dungy had won a Super Bowl with the Indianapolis Colts, but is better remembered for his determination to demand high character from his players. Coach Dungy persuaded Vick to eliminate his neighborhood friends from his advisory council and put Coach Dungy at the head of it instead. Through Coach Dungy's mentoring, Vick survived jail and managed to get back to the NFL and once again become a starting quarterback. Though Vick's reputation has forever been scarred, his story is an example of how anything is possible when you place good people on your personal team.

As an exercise, take a moment and write down the roles you derived from the questions above. Next, think of the names and phone numbers of those people who will fill the most important roles on your team. It might be wise to think of more than one person for each role since you haven't officially confirmed that anyone will voluntarily help you. As you write down each name, think about why that person would want to help you. Your coach, for example, wants to see you be successful, but he also wants to win. You have a shared interest. Your parents may want you to have the best experience possible. After all, they paid money to the organization for you to have a positive experience. A school tutor might get paid by the school to help students because he is looking into a career in teaching. Your strength trainer enjoys human anatomy and, though he may or not get paid, he enjoys helping athletes discover their physical potential.

Often times a person's interest is non-sports related, and that's alright. They just want to see you succeed as a person. A grandparent, for example, might want to offer advice on how to organize your schedule, while a friend may want to keep you in check when it comes to relationships. Still, it's important to clarify their interest in you. It may be simply because they like you and want to help. However, thinking about what they want will help you in the recruiting process.

Finally, think of ways that you can reciprocate. For example, doing your chores at home will make your parents extremely happy. Spending time with your grandparents also makes them proud. Maybe your friend is doing a car wash fundraiser and needs some help. You may want to think about washing a few cars for him. Your coach wants to know that you are staying out of trouble and staying eligible. Go out of your way to let him know that you're working hard off the field as well as on it to help build the reputation of the program. Perhaps offer to give speeches around the community to help with your program's marketing so more players will want to play for your team. Remember, the more you are willing to help others, the more they are willing to help you.

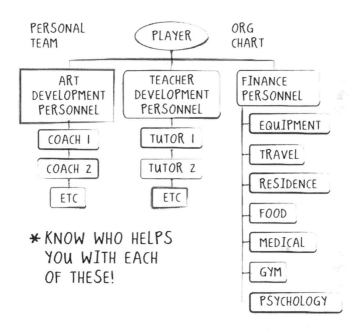

Once you have your list, you'll want to approach all the people on it and let them know your athletic goals, both short and long term. Let them know that you'd be honored if they would fill a role for you, and that you've thought about ways you could help them in return. Let them know what you've thought about. However—and this is important—ask them if there is a different way, other than what you've thought about, that they would like to have you reciprocate. This shows that you are listening and that you care about them. It also builds your relationship with that person. If they mention something different, decide whether you can agree to help in that manner. If you can agree, make sure you do it. This builds trust, and it's extremely important when recruiting your personal team.

Building this trust with your personal team will protect and help you in ways you can't even imagine until a situation comes up. Perhaps you'll have an injury. Having a personal team will get you back on the field ready to play much more quickly than doing it all on your own. Perhaps you will have a difficult class that threatens your eligibility. Having a team will help guide you through that difficulty so that you finish the class and receive passing grades. Perhaps you enter a dating relationship that is distracting you and affecting your focus during practice. Your team will recognize this and get you out of the clouds and back to earth.

Throughout this book, I've tried to pinpoint many examples that could get in the way of your athletic focus, but I'm not going to know all of the details of what pops up in your personal experience. Building your personal team around you will help you respond to your own specific challenges. Having a solid personal team will help you make more right decisions than wrong ones. Your job now, though, is to make sure you have a solid personal team to help you with everything you need.

# CHAPTER 15
## The Draft

IT WAS A HOT JULY DAY, and we came down to the last pick during the draft. Everyone knew that we'd wind up with the youngest, heaviest, slowest, least athletic kid in the draft. One coach said he was a "killer." This kid's parents were worried about his not being involved in sports, so they decided to sign him up for football. He hadn't done any other sport prior. Our head coach had determined that this kid wouldn't last, and he thought that was a good thing. The logic was that if he quit, we could start a more athletic player in his place. So, we drafted him, and we would see how he did during practice.

On our first day of practice he asked, "Does anybody else smell pork chops?" I shook my head because I knew he had just given himself a nickname. A few days later, we went into hitting. "Porkchop" carried the ball, stood straight up, and was hit right in the stomach. He went down hard, and coaches across the field could hear him grunt with the air coming right out of him. Porkchop rolled over in agony, and the head coach told him to get out of the drill. The head coach figured showing him no mercy would certainly tell Porkchop that football was not the sport for him.

However, to his credit, Porkchop got up and went to the back of the line to do it again. I smiled because he was not going to be run off. As time went on, I worked with Porkchop to understand the game. He began the season for us as a defensive lineman but moved to offensive guard. He became a valuable backside guard protector for us. As the season progressed, we went undefeated through the regular season. During one game when we scored a bunch, we gave the ball to Porkchop. He was immediately hit at the line of scrimmage, but he kept his legs going and fell forward across the goal line for a two-point conversion. All the other players were so excited for him; you could see them jump up and down when they knew he had some points.

We remained undefeated and went on to win the championship. A few weeks after the game, we held our end-of-season party. At one point during the party, while all the players were running around and playing video games, Porkchop walked by our head coach. Our head coach said, "Well, Porkchop. What do you think?"

Porkchop surprised him when he said, "I'm just glad I have one more day to be with my teammates again." Porkchop was only nine years old, but at that moment he was the teacher and we were the students.

After you and your parents make your selection as to which youth program you are going to play in, your parents will then write the association a check, you'll pick up your equipment, and you'll be ready for tryouts. Wait a minute. Have you wondered why there is a tryout to begin with?

If you said, "Because there is a draft," you're right. When there are multiple players in an association, the association doesn't want to turn away players because they want to make sure they collect the checks. With more money, they can make the association better. However, the league rules will limit the number of players per team, just to make things even. Thus, the association will take the number of players that signed up, divide that number by the number of players allowed per team, and that will tell them how many teams they have. If there are extra players, they will add one more team, but the association will even things out by limiting its teams to fewer than the league minimum. They do this in case a few more players sign up to play later. This way they will have room to allow more players to enter the association. Remember, more players means more money to attract more players.

As signups happen, the association works to anticipate how many head coaches they will need by the number of players signed up. Many times an association anticipates correctly, and the athletic director and board members interview potential head coaches during the off-season. If they have enough head coaches, great! However, if they don't, then the recruiting process begins. Remember, they want to look for head coaches who will pass certain qualifications first. In the end, though, they'll take anybody willing to put in the time, because they would rather qualify a poor head coach than turn away players who have parents who write checks. Thus, if there is high demand for a good program, you may still run the risk of playing for a poor coach. If you do, this is usually why it happens.

The goal of the association is to have head coaches determined before tryouts. Many of these coaches are parents of players. Obviously, a coach's son or daughter won't get drafted by another team, so the association puts rules on how many coaches' sons are "locked down" during draft day. For example, association rules may prohibit six coaches who all have sons from getting together and forming one dominant team. The association may only allow two coaches to join forces, and then everyone else is fair game.

During tryouts, the goal of each head coach is to rank players so he can determine who he wants to draft. Obviously, if he gets the first pick, he'll want to pick up who he thinks is the best player available. If he gets the second pick, he'll want to pick the second best player, all the way down the player list until the last player is picked. But if the coach has a son or daughter playing, that player will have to be a "selection" in a round. Where that player is drafted in the round is cause for all kinds of arguments on draft day.

Believe it or not, the head coach with his child as a player will suddenly become the most humble of dads in the draft room and say that his son is a mid-rounder at best. He might even go so far as to say that his child can't even tie his own shoes. Sure, he intends to use his son as the starting quarterback or running back, but he wants to convince everyone else that his son is a horrible player in order to get another strong player for his team.

On the other hand, all the other head coaches will say that this coach's son is absolutely the best player ever to wear a uniform! In fact, he could sign a college scholarship at 12 years old! They want to make sure that the coach doesn't get a first-round pick! Some head coaches sign their kids up and then don't bring them for try-outs, solely for the purpose of preventing the other head coaches from ranking them. If they do bring their kids for tryouts, often times they tell them not to play hard, or even to play poorly, only so that they can try to convince the other coaches that they need a first-round pick to be competitive. These arguments go on in every draft room around the country, and the one that finally makes a decision is the athletic director.

Another thing that can happen is that a group of players might decide not to show up at tryouts. Their dads are not coaching, so they are fair game. However, their not being at tryouts makes it difficult for other coaches to rank them, and therefore difficult to want to select them. Then, all of a sudden during draft day, a head coach starts drafting all the players that didn't show up at tryouts. What happened is that this head coach knew who many of the best players were and called their parents before tryouts. He told them to stay home during tryouts so that he could make sure all of them were on his team. The parents were okay with this because they paid money and wanted their sons to be on the winning team. Everyone was in on it. I knew one baseball head coach who did this. He put together such an athletic and dominant team that no one could even come close to them during the season. Yes, they won the championship, but the association changed the rules after this so that it wouldn't happen again.

I've seen many other things happen in a draft room. I've seen a head coach and board member get replaced during draft day, and I was torn from another team to replace that head coach. I've seen head coaches show up with another dad who was not the registered assistant. Remember the "two-coach rule" I talked about earlier? This head coach was trying to get three coaches, and thus three play-ers. He was daring the other head coaches to draft this dad's son. Seeing as how nobody wanted to draft a player who didn't want to play for them, the other coaches let this head coach get away with it. However, what goes around comes around. The head coach's advantage quickly evaporated when his star player was hurt, and their season finished mediocre at best.

Finally, when the end of the draft order approaches, I've seen head coaches draft kids simply with the hope that they could run them off when the season starts. Youth football often has a "clear the bench" rule, meaning everyone gets to go in the game when there is a change in possession. If a player is drafted last, coaches will call that player a "killer," meaning his playing is going to kill whichever team he is on. The idea is to run a player off so that more of the better players will get to play. I am personally opposed to this approach during draft day, and I would admonish any coach who would do this. The coach's job is to develop players and to teach teamwork. Yes, it can take more work, but I've seen too many times the reward that comes with taking a "killer" and making him into an all-star. Still, your association's draft room may have head coaches who feel this way, and it's good to be aware that this goes on. Your parents may want to ask the association about what they do in this situation.

When you are selected to a team, it's good to know what happened during the draft. If a team appears overly dominant, especially early in the season, it could be because a head coach was able to manipulate the association into getting better players. A team like this is not unbeatable, but every player on your team will have to be at his best when playing a team of good athletes. As goes a common saying among coaches, "Your team can lose with good players, but your team can't win without them."

Winning championships is another matter. If you and your teammates work on your ART (Alignment, Rules, Technique) and play together as a team, by the end of the season, you'll have every chance of beating that team and taking home the trophy.

In his books, Head Coach Lou Holtz loves to tell the story about his football team getting ready to play in the Orange Bowl. It was a big game against a tough opponent. Right before the game, however, two of his best players violated team rules, and Lou Holtz sent them both home. The players on his team were unsettled. Playing against a tough opponent, they felt uneasy about losing two of their best players.

Coach Holtz called a team meeting. Worried about the attitude of his team, he told them that he wanted them to speak up. But he didn't want them to talk about why they couldn't win. Instead, he wanted them to talk about why they could. Before long, players stood up talking about how they had great linemen, a great QB, a history of playing together, and a terrific defense. Ultimately, Coach Holtz's team changed their attitude, and on the field of battle they emerged victorious. His team pulled off a terrific upset, but the only people who thought they could win were themselves.

What goes on in a preseason draft increases the odds of winning. However, wins and losses are only determined by what happens on the field on game day. Upsets happen regularly because teams come together at exactly the right moment, while other teams take for granted what they have. No matter what happens in your draft, if you and your teammates work together, stay focused, and believe in yourselves, anything is possible. Thus, as the saying goes, "That's why they play the game."

Ultimately, politics is part of the sports game. You need to be aware of what happens behind closed doors and protect yourself by selecting a good organization to play for. Also, understand what kind of coach you play for and build a dedicated personal team intent upon your success. Doing these things gives you the best chance to focus on your ART, and will thus allow you to develop your career.

# PART III

## RELATIONSHIPS

# CHAPTER 16

## Your Opponent

**I'LL NEVER FORGET THE WESTERN GAME** in 1992. Western had a great team made up of very good athletes. The Monday before the game, our head coach called the offense into our regular formation and had us stand there as he told us who we were going to line up against. I was a junior offensive guard, standing barely 6' tall and weighing only 195 pounds. Coach announced that the guy playing over me was a wide defensive tackle who stood 5'11" and weighed 280 pounds. He was a senior and he was going to be very difficult to move. I was going to have my work cut out for me.

Fortunately, I was very confident in my blocking Technique from what my father taught me, but I knew that it would be important to learn a few other tricks just in case. All that week I worked on cut blocking so that I could keep him honest. If he didn't know which way I was going to hit him, I would stand a better chance of keeping him off balance. As the week progressed, I mixed up my blocking during scrimmages, going both high and low on my opponent. By the time Friday came around, I felt I was ready. Between classes that day, one of the girls in school asked me, "Aren't we playing Western today?" When I told her that we were, she looked at me sadly and said, "You guys are going to get killed." I laughed, thanked her for believing in us, and used it as additional motivation.

At seven o'clock, kickoff at Western High School ensued. We received the ball and went on offense. There he was, lined up in front of me. He looked to me like he was just as wide as he was tall. He also looked strong. I found out later that he was also a very good heavyweight wrestler. Coach called the first play right over him. As I shot out to hit him, I literally bounced off of him. He hit our running back but failed to bring him down right away, and we managed a four-yard gain. The next play, I went at him again, this time going for his legs. He fell over me, and I realized that the strategy of mixing up my blocking would wear him out.

Again and again I went after him. Over time, I realized that he was getting worn down. Shortly thereafter, he went out of the game, and his backup came in. I looked up to see that my new opponent was their starting left tackle. He stood at 6'5" and over 300 pounds. "Okay," I said to myself. "Same strategy. Different opponent." By the third quarter, they were rotating between the two at defensive tackle. It was a tight ball game, but we could see that they were wearing down.

Finally, on a play in the fourth quarter, I looked up and saw that they had put in their third string defensive tackle. This kid was 6'1", but he looked to be only about 180 pounds. I remember thinking to myself, "This guy's toast," and after that next play he was injured and asked the coaches if he could to come to the sideline. One and done.

Strangely, I remember my father yelling at me on the sideline. He sent out my substitute and took me off the field. Even though I took out that defensive tackle, I didn't follow my Rules. I was supposed to pull left and hit the inside linebacker, but I was so focused on taking out the defensive tackle that I missed my assignment. Dad said that we could have scored a touchdown on that play had I not been selfish. Even though I tried to make the argument, "But they don't have any more defensive tackles," he had me sit out the rest of the series. Ultimately, we did score a touchdown to take the lead, and when the final buzzer sounded, our team won the game. It was a big upset that made the local papers.

I have an award for being the offensive player of the week during that Western game, but that's not what I remember. The lessons I learned that week made me realize that no matter who I was playing against, I had a chance to help the team win as long as I executed my ART. With help from my coaches, I implemented a strategy that used my opponents' strengths against them. Practicing that strategy added confidence to what I was doing. During the game I made a mistake at one point of not following my Rules in the ART concept, but I increased the odds of our winning by having great Technique.

As the weeks progressed, it wasn't going to get any easier. My next opponents were 275 lbs, 295 lbs, and 250 lbs, and all of them were extremely strong. They all wanted to use their size against me, but speed and quickness allowed me to compete. It wasn't until the last game of the season that I ran into trouble. Clark High School had a talented team with several Division I prospects. In front of me was a guy named Ahaz Griffeth. He was about 6'0" and weighed 220. Unlike some of the other defensive linemen I played against who were bigger and stronger than I was, Ahaz knew Technique and how to use his hands. He understood leverage and had a very high energy level, never quitting and always hustling. After the first few plays, I knew I was in for a fight. Ahaz wasn't a player I could just outsmart. He was a player who made me be my absolute best.

When you play sports, you will have an opponent to compete against. While some sports don't involve physical contact with an opponent, their mere willingness to compete raises a bar that you must overcome. Of course, physical contact with an opponent will test you in other ways as well. In either case, you have to have a strategy, practice your ART, and then be able to execute in the heat of the moment. If it weren't for your opponent pushing you to be your best, you could get away with a lesser effort. However, because an opponent creates a risk of losing as well as a chance for winning, you'll be driven to be the best you can be simply because he's there. Conversely, if you don't strive to be your best, your opponent will walk away with the win, and you'll soon walk away to another afternoon activity.

Regardless of the personality of your opponent, he or she is going to have certain strengths and weaknesses. Sometimes those strengths and weaknesses are physical. However, more often than not those strengths and weaknesses are mental. A common phrase among college coaches is, "Everyone's on scholarship." That means that just about all programs will have a good weight program, competitive coaches, and a good nutrition program. Where athletes differ, however, is in the attitude and the spirit in which they play.

I remember specifically asking my father about who was the best player he played against. His answer somewhat surprised me because he mentioned a player I had never heard of before. However, there was a different player who had a big reputation among the press and even had some celebrity status during the same era, so I asked my dad about him.

"He couldn't take pain," he said. I thought his answer was fascinating. In order to find a weakness so specific, and one that is more mental than physical at that, and then to be able to exploit it in the heat of the moment is truly delving into the depths of a tactical strategy against an opponent.

I then had to ask my father what made the other player so good. "He was smart," he said. "You couldn't keep doing the same things against him. You had to mix it up to keep him guessing, while he'd try to do the same to you. It was a chess match." Dad taught me a valuable lesson that day. When looking at an opponent, you have to think through strategy as you practice your ART. Dad's ability to do this awarded him the chance to go to eight Pro Bowls and twice receive the Seagrams Crown of Sports award for being the NFL's best offensive lineman. His awards were not an accident. He proved that you can't just win physically. You have to win mentally as well.

The good news is that there are only so many things an opponent can do to try to beat you. If you can identify what those things are, prepare to recognize them on the field, and then have a plan to exploit them, you are well on your way to a victory. An opposing pitcher, for example, might have a poor curve ball, a decent fast ball, but a really mean breaking ball. Maybe all he practices are his fast balls and his breaking balls, and that's why those are his best pitches. If you can recognize those pitches before the ball leaves his hand, you have a shot at eliminating his strength. What's more, if that strength is eliminated, he'll try his curve ball, and you already know he's not very good at those. If you take away his strength, he'll know he's in a position of weakness, and then you can exploit it.

Interestingly enough, most athletes don't think in these terms. They are so insecure about their own weaknesses that they don't bother to try to find out about their opponents' weaknesses. When this happens, an athlete will respond in one of two ways: either he'll be timid or he'll be aggressive. It's the "fight or flight" reaction.

First, he may be timid. The fear of the unknown as well as the knowledge of his own weaknesses will make him insecure, and he won't play with any confidence. He will lose before he ever takes the field. Second, he may be aggressive. He'll focus on his strengths and play with reckless abandon. This is obviously the better of the two outcomes, but he runs a risk of playing into his opponent's strengths. Usually this is what happens when an athlete gives all of his best effort but fails to come away with a victory. When undirected aggression fails to bring a victory, an athlete can't help but be discouraged.

Fortunately, there is a simple method that can help begin to overcome this, and that is observation. The more you observe your opponent, the more familiar you will become with his tendencies. This is the advantage of undertaking hours of film study. I never really realized how much this was true until I took a trip to play the Stanford Cardinal my senior year in college. Sitting in a team meeting room on Thursday night, somehow I had overlooked that injuries had raised my status to second string on the depth chart. It never occurred to me that I might actually have to play a significant role, and because the injuries came late I realized I needed to watch film of Stanford quickly.

While my teammates relaxed on Friday, I put in seven hours of film study on the Stanford offense. It wasn't long before I could recognize which plays they would run out of which formations. In fact, it was almost funny how predictable they actually were. When the game began, I stood on the sidelines watching their offense come out in their predictable fashion. They didn't do anything different from the seven hours of film I watched the day before. In fact, I was calling out the plays from the sideline before the ball was snapped.

Sadly, we didn't win, and I didn't get in the game, but I learned from that day that an opponent only has so much time to practice certain things, and in order to master them they have to do them repetitively. That repetitiveness makes them vulnerable if you can eliminate their strengths and force them to do things with which they are uncomfortable. I heard this again when I was coaching high school football with a future state championship coach. We were talking about defense, and he mentioned that one of his mentors told him to find the three things an offense liked best, and take those three things away. If he could do that, odds were the offense would never score a point.

Once again, there are only so many ways an opponent will try to gain an advantage. Usually, an opponent will gravitate towards those ways with which he is most comfortable. These are usually the Alignments, Rules, and Techniques that he practices on a regular basis. Take a look at your opponent and see if you can identify his ART. What are the top three things he's good at doing? Write those down on a piece of paper.

Now, is there anything about his Alignment, Rules, or Techniques that you can exploit or change that will make him uncomfortable and expose a weakness? Can you get him out of Alignment? Does he ever hesitate because he's not sure of his Rules? Is there a Technique he uses in certain situations that shows vulnerability? Write all these down as well.

Finally, take a look at your own ART, and determine if there is a way you can direct your ART into exploiting these weaknesses. Your coach should help you in this endeavor. Perhaps his poor Alignment will give you an opportunity you can exploit. Maybe his Rule hesitation will give you a chance to go after him aggressively. Is he lazy with any of his Techniques? Whatever it is you wish to exploit, practice these things so that they become comfortable for you. As Knute Rockne once said, "Work on your weaknesses until they become your strengths." If there is anything you know you can exploit but you yourself are uncomfortable doing, then work to make it comfortable. These items will then become your ART when you perform in competition. The more you exploit your opponent's weaknesses and play into your strengths, the greater chance you and your team will have at victory!

# CHAPTER 17
## Injuries

**SPORTS IS A PHYSICAL ENDEAVOR.** And because physics is involved, the human body bends and contorts in all sorts of ways. Sometimes, physics goes against the human body and injury happens. When you play sports, it's not a question of *if* you get injured, but *when*. Because of this, I felt it would be important to dedicate a chapter on injury.

An injury can happen for any number of reasons. Sometimes a player can make a spectacular self-sacrificing play on behalf of his team, as Notre Dame running back Reggie Brooks did when he was knocked out crossing the end zone in a game against Michigan. On other occasions, it can happen for no apparent reason at all, as a teammate of mine experienced on his way to a walk-through when he stepped on the indoor practice field. When his foot hit the Astroturf, his ankle popped and instantly he was out for the season. Done. Sadly, I've also seen it happen during non-team activities, such as when an athlete acts recklessly during a party or drives irresponsibly. Too often non-team activities involving alcohol or drugs end in someone getting seriously hurt or even killed. Because athletes have more experience controlling their bodies, they tend to think they can overcome inebriation. In reality, no one is invincible, and one moment of lack of judgment can end your career or your life.

Regardless of how injuries occur, they all have three things in common. First, there is physical pain. The body is damaged. It needs to heal. Pain is the body's way of telling you not to do that anymore. Second, however, there is emotional pain. There is a separation from your ART and that part of yourself. For some period of time you will not be able to be a performer. There is also a separation from your teammates out on the field. They will have to adjust to your not being there to help. Third, there is concern among the people you've selected to help you as an athlete, such as your personal team, parents, coaches, tutors, fans, etc. Many people can suffer as a result of an injury. However, how you handle your injury will tell you about your own character.

When an injury occurs, you'll know it by your pain or your mobility. If a part of your body doesn't work, there's something physically wrong and it needs to be evaluated. Sometimes pain is just a part of being an athlete and you should play through it. If you're sore but the body still works, you can still compete. Conversely, if you're experiencing pain and you can't bend a certain way, more than likely you'll need to see a medical professional. The same holds true for non-apparent injuries such as concussions. Pain in and of itself isn't bad, but if the body fails to work at all it's time to see your medical professional.

The goal of your medical professional is to get you healed and back on the field as quickly as possible without risking re-injury to the affected area. The best cases are when you can wrap tape around the affected area for support and you can continue playing. Other cases involve a period of rest before you can return. However, more serious injuries can require surgery and rehab on your part before the medical professional will clear you to return. Rehab is the targeted strengthening and breaking down of the scar tissue of an affected area. This is done again in order to avoid the risk of re-injury.

Finally, and especially for those athletes with long careers, a medical professional may make a recommendation that it's time to "hang up your cleats," meaning that your body just can't continue to perform the way it used to and you need to stop playing your sport or risk a far worse outcome. As my father once wrote in the *New York Times* in 1979 when discussing an injury that would threaten his career, "The bottom dropped out of my world; I felt tears and a rise in body temperature as I realized I was going to lose the ability to do what I enjoyed doing best." I, too, heard a doctor and a coach tell me to quit playing and to have a nice life after experiencing a bad back injury. When so much of what you do identifies who you are, and you can no longer do what you love to do, you go through a period where you struggle with who you are.

And this, then, is the second challenge. While you are stuck in a room with your leg in a cast, your teammates and your competition are out on the field practicing their ART and getting ready to perform. They are learning, taking in new experiences, and forming new bonds while you have to do repetitive rehab on your joint. Your coaches might be giving opportunities to another player who just replaced you on the depth chart. If you're thinking all this and more when you're injured, you need to stop and re-evaluate your worth as a human being.

Let me explain. Everything I mentioned above may be true. You are experiencing a separation from the team in activity, and your coaches dropped you from the depth chart. Yes, your competition is getting better while they are practicing and gaining experience. However, if it's all about you, and you're worried about your opportunities, you've never quite grasped the spirit of what it means to be a team in the first place. This holds true just as much in individual sports as it does in team sports. Winning isn't an "I" thing. It's a "we" thing. Everybody working together makes a team, whether you're the star player or the water boy. No one is more important than anyone else. Just because you may be injured doesn't mean you're no longer a part of the team, whether your team is composed of other athletes or simply consists of your parents. In fact, now's your chance to prove that it's about the team by contributing in ways that are different from how you've contributed before.

When you're injured, your job is to get back on the field as quickly as you can. However, there is only so much rehab you should do. Much of what the body needs is pure rest. That doesn't mean, though, that you can't help contribute. If you truly believe in the idea of a team, you'll find ways to make others better. Are you worried about your backup taking your spot? I've got news for you. If you help coach him, when you return, you'll be a better player.

How do I know this? Simply put, you'll see the game from a different perspective. When you learn from someone else's mistakes, you'll see not only your own areas you need to improve on, but you'll also see the effects that those mistakes will have on the team as a whole. Knowing "why" something needs to be done a certain way solidifies within the athlete the desire to do it the right way, especially under the pressure of competition. The more mentally you get involved in the game, the more wisdom you'll have when you step back on the field. Then, when you have the "why" firmly grasped from helping your teammates, the game will slow down for you with your new perspective.

So, while you are recovering from an injury, you need to recognize that you are still a part of the team. Then you need to act as though you are a part of it. Be diligent in your rehab efforts and rest. Focus on strengthening your core and your joints so that re-injury does not occur. Watch as much film as you can, both of your own games as well as those of upcoming opponents. Write down those times when your ART was good, as well as those times when it could have been better. Resolve mentally to improve your ART, and if you aren't sure why something happened in the past, ask your coach for help so you can be sure to correct it when you get back on the field. Look at the ART of your team's future opponents, and see if you can determine their strengths and weaknesses. Analyze their ART and determine how best to attack them. Finally, attend all practices. Take what you know and help your teammates while they practice, all the while grasping why the ART needs to be done a certain way.

Finally, when you're all healed up and you're back on the field, you'll come to that moment when you'll need to develop confidence in your healed injury. It needs to be tested. Fortunately, with all the work and strengthening you've done, and with all the focus you've put on Alignment, Rules, and Technique, you'll be in a position to perform better and with greater ease than you may have done prior to getting injured.

And that's the best part. Usually injuries occur because we try too hard doing things the wrong way. Once we put our focus back on doing things the right way, letting the game come to us rather than trying to force it, the game becomes easier and more enjoyable.

What we'll also find is that while competition drives us to want to achieve more physically than anyone else, in reality not all of our bodies are built the same. Yes, a weight is a weight and a lift is a lift when training. However, sometimes one athlete's arms may be longer than another's, and he'll have to press the same amount of weight farther. Sometimes an athlete's legs will have one running mechanic overcompensate for another while sprinting.

For myself, being the son of an eight-time NFL Pro Bowler who stood at 6'5", I spent my time trying to grow up to be athletically just like my father. However, God had other plans and only let me grow to be 6'0" tall (depending on who does the measurement). As hard as it was to take that I wasn't going to grow anymore, I made a conscious decision to outwork everyone in the weight room, trying to lift as much as I could all the time. You could call it "undirected aggression" in my own training. As we talked about before, undirected aggression is better than being timid, but it leaves us vulnerable.

It wasn't until I was injured from my training and couldn't work out that I had to rethink how I trained. Forget trying to keep up with everyone else. Heck, I couldn't even walk, let alone run. At that moment, I made a new conscious decision to set goals for my own body. Often in the past I didn't always use the best form while training. From now on, I was going to focus on my form, and if I didn't feel I had complete control of the weight, I wouldn't increase it until I felt I had complete control. At the same time, I was going to look hard at my diet. Having a voracious appetite, which often comes with a high metabolism, I was known for eating just about anything in sight. From that point on, I would only focus on those things that had the best nutritional value. I was going to appreciate my body for how God made it. I didn't want to try to be someone else anymore. I was going to focus on being the best me I could be for the sake of my team.

It wasn't easy at first. I was separated from my team, doing rehab, scaling back my weight training, and starting over. It appeared to be wishful thinking that I would ever see the field again. However, after a month of getting into it, I noticed that things came easier. In fact, I was getting stronger more quickly than I had before. When it all came back, I felt bigger, stronger, and faster than I ever was before I was injured, and that's because I was. Granted I would never be the 6'5" superstar, but I was no less important and I was better than I was before because of what I experienced with my injury.

Injuries often give us much needed humility at the time we need it most. As Proverbs says, "With the humble is wisdom found." When you have an injury, the strength of your character and the strength of your team will be tested. When you make it through that test, you will be much stronger as a person, and your team will be stronger in the face of competition. Knowing that you are no less important and that you are facing your injury with the right attitude will inspire your teammates as well as help you understand what others are going through when they have their own injuries.

In closing, one year I was a head coach of a youth football team. Midway through the season, my left guard injured his ankle, and he was going to be out for the remainder of the year. I mentioned to the player as well as the parents that he was still a part of this team, and we wanted him to come and help coach and be a part of it. To my surprise, the parents decided it was not worth it, and we never saw the player again. I was saddened because we were all in this together, and I cared about the player. What's worse, as he grew up in life, I wondered what lessons he would learn regarding his value to a team.

Conversely, during a different season, one of our athletes suffered a broken arm during the first day of practice, and he was going to be out the rest of the year. This kid's father, however, knew that his son would be a part of the team, and together they made a commitment to come to every practice and every game for the entire season. I know it wasn't easy, but that athlete held true to his commitment. During practices he helped with drills, passed out water, and did whatever else we asked of him. Our team won every game that season, and he was there in uniform the entire time.

At the end of the season, we won the championship. Even though he never played a snap, he was a true champion because he helped the team every step of the way. When we held our end-of-the-year party, he was there to get his trophy. When the league recognized the winners with their names on the big board by the main field, his name was up there with those of his teammates. Finally, because we coaches were so excited to win, the head coach bought championship rings for all the players. He received one, too, and no one can take it away from him.

If you compare the actions and attitudes of these two players, which one do you think learned the valuable lesson? I can tell you that the first player did not show up in our league to play again, but the second came back and continued to play. One walked away from his commitment to his team, while the other stayed committed and became a champion.

In the end, know that your value to your team is not your athletic ability. It's the talents God put inside you to contribute to the cause whichever way you can to help your team. When you're injured, you still have value. As Head Coach Lou Holtz always told us, "People can accomplish great things if enough people care!" Be more committed to helping your team when you're injured, and you, too, will still have the chance to be a champion!

# CHAPTER 18
## Outside Relationships

**WHILE MY FATHER WAS STILL IN THE NFL**, he was part owner of a sports bar in Phoenix, Arizona. One night while he was working, a customer in the corner started telling stories about how he and my father were the best of friends. "George Kunz and I go way back!" he would say. "Our wives are friends and they go shopping together, and he and I get on the golf course a couple of times a month. In fact, there was one time..." and the stories would go on and on. Eventually, a few of the other customers gathered around to hear, and my dad went over to hear some of the stories as well. Dad had no idea who this guy was. But he sat there quietly to hear what he would say.

Eventually, the customer looked at my dad and said, "Hey, you're a big feller. What's your name?"

"Well actually," my dad replied, "I'm George Kunz."

There was silence. After a few chuckles, the other customers went back to the bar, and the storyteller paid his tab sheepishly and sneaked out of the bar.

I say this to tell you that if you're going to be an athlete, you need to know that people will respond differently to you, if only because you have chosen to represent your team. With this choice you have made, people who are not on your team will look at you differently than they do others who haven't made that choice. They will form an early opinion of you whether you know it or not.

For example, if you are in school, other students who don't play sports will form an opinion of you. One friend of mine, for example, decided that she didn't like all the football players that played for her high school because of the way they acted in the cafeteria. Granted, probably not all the football players misbehaved. But because a few did, her perception put all of the players on the team in the same category, and she formulated a negative opinion about all football players.

At the other extreme, such as the case with the storyteller, some people will want to be friends with athletes so much that they might make up stories about it. You never really know how people will behave until they actually do.

So, what we're really talking about here are your outside relationships. These are people outside of your athletic and personal team. They are not people who have offered to help with your athletic career. These can consist of family members, friends, dating relationships, students, fans, etc. How you choose to handle, or not handle, these relationships can have a major impact on your athletic career. What's also true is that these outside relationships can hurt an entire team if they are not handled properly by the athlete.

Poorly managed outside relationships can have varying degrees of consequences. I knew of several very talented athletes on my football team in high school who didn't play to their potential because they were more concerned about the girls they were dating. When some of us felt they could have had opportunities to go to the next level, their mediocre playing closed the door on that opportunity.

Other athletes I know slacked off from studying because they were goofing off with friends. There's nothing wrong with spending time with friends, but if you let that get in the way of your overall objectives, you run the risk of becoming academically ineligible, which then hurts you and your team.

Often times poorly managed relationships end in a very embarrassing situation for the athlete, and that can spill over onto the team. The most recent public example of this would be the events that transpired at Notre Dame prior to their playing Alabama in the 2013 National Championship Game. As the team rallied around star inside linebacker Manti Te'o during their undefeated season, the press ran story after story about how he played inspirationally after the death of his girlfriend in California. Strangely, when the regular season was over, the dead girlfriend called Te'o out of the blue. Needless to say, something was strange. Calling it a very poorly managed outside relationship doesn't even come close to doing it justice.

The events that later transpired could be read in the papers, and you can form your own opinions about what to believe. Nonetheless, when that happened, it affected the Notre Dame locker room as well as Te'o. As the players came out on national television, I could see it in their faces, though at the time I didn't know what had happened. The timing couldn't have been worse, as the Notre Dame team needed to be totally focused for a very tough opponent in the championship game. The results that night spoke for themselves. Alabama won the game in a blowout. Thus, even a seemingly innocent relationship, though poorly managed, can hurt an entire team.

On a more serious note, higher degrees of consequences from poorly managed relationships are usually seen in the sports section when an athlete gets arrested. On many occasions, an athlete will be with "friends" who choose to break the law and convince the athlete to "join in the fun." Many times these athletes are pressured into alcohol, sex, or drugs from "friends" who "mean no harm." If they were truly friends, they would be helping the athlete's career, not putting it at risk.

Therefore, you will want to think about setting up ground rules for your outside relationships. It's okay to have outside relationships. However, not having any ground rules leaves you, your athletic career, and your team vulnerable to choices you may make in a moment of weakness. Just like everything before, you need to have a plan.

Your first step when formulating a plan is to identify where you need help on your personal team. It's best to determine how you will proceed up front, and if someone wants to be a true friend of yours, he might want a place on your personal team. If all your positions are filled, there's nothing wrong with making room for someone. Just know that at some point he may be asking for a favor from you. If he wants to help, it's best to determine what he wants for helping you. If he says "nothing," that's fine. Just remember that if he asks for help in the future, he told you "nothing." This doesn't mean that you don't have to help him. It just means that you will help him because you want to, not as a return for a favor. Thus, it's important to determine the terms of the agreement up front. This way there's no room for error, and just like a team, you will all be on the same page.

If you have friends who don't want to help, but you enjoy spending time with them, it's best to let them know that your time will be limited, and there will be times when you'll need to be working on your athletic career. Most of the time they will say, "That's fine," and everything will be okay. However, if they try to talk you into doing things that could be reckless, you need to remember your ground rules.

One of the hardest things to do can be to walk away from people. Remember, though, that you're not walking away from someone or something. You're walking towards someone or something else. There's always a choice. If someone tries to pull you into something that you know can put you at risk, think of the things that you want and work for, and walk towards them. When the right idea is in your mind, the wrong idea won't have any room, and it will be easier to walk towards what is best for you.

Ultimately, what we're talking about here is temptation, and having the wisdom to determine if you are being tempted. The world is full of great and inspiring people who have fallen due to temptation. Don't think you will be any different, because all the ones who fell thought that they would be different, too. The best plan of attack to protect yourself is to develop some ground rules, figure out the roles you want people to play, and then manage your outside relationships according to those ground rules and roles. If you can create a support structure around you of people who love you and care about you, they will be your best defense from those who want to tempt you.

There was a time when my father met a friend who used to play for the New York Jets. After a while, they began hanging out. Upon meeting him, however, my mother became somewhat suspicious. What's more, this new character liked to hang out in questionable places around town. My mother was concerned about it and eventually voiced her discomfort around him to my dad. Dad took it into consideration but didn't do anything about it right away.

There's an old saying that if you want to get to know someone, take a trip with him. Well, Dad, this guy, and a few other friends went away for a weekend on a golf trip. When they came back, something happened that made Dad understand what my mother was seeing. Dad decided that she was right and that he wasn't going to spend any more time with the former Jet.

But wait, it gets worse. We later found out that this former Jet didn't ever play for the Jets at all. He was a guy impersonating a former player for the New York Jets. He had fake IDs made, opened accounts in his name, and was running a double life. This guy so much wanted to be an NFL player that he decided to impersonate one. Plus, he was willing to break the law to do it! My mother was very wise in how she handled that situation, and her wisdom, her courage, and her prayers helped my dad when he could have been in danger.

Another friend of mine from Notre Dame was Renaldo Wynn. Renaldo was a talented defensive lineman from Chicago who while in college met a girlfriend in Las Vegas. As I also lived in Las Vegas at the time, I was able to show him around town and we would train in the offseason together. At one point while we were training, he looked up at the clock and exclaimed that he had to make a phone call. I realized that he was going to call his girlfriend, Latanya, so I joked saying, "Tell her, 'Don't pay the ransom! I've escaped!'" My dad used to say this to my mom when he was calling her in the same fashion.

Being the son of a professional athlete, I knew what was happening. Renaldo's girlfriend wanted to make sure that good things happened to him, but she also knew that there were temptations that would come to him if he wasn't careful. Thus, they had an agreement to keep in touch just to make sure everything was alright.

It worked out because Renaldo was later drafted in the first round by the Jacksonville Jaguars and had a long career. I know she had her work cut out for her during that time, though, after a conversation he and I had in Jacksonville at dinner. I asked him what he noticed about guys getting into the NFL. He said, "You know, it's strange. Half the guys that get drafted are so appreciative to get to the NFL that they don't want to do anything to screw it up. Most of us spend our fun evenings out bowling or helping charities with our wives. The other half, though, see things differently. They want to live it up and go absolutely wild. They party all night and spend like crazy. I don't know how they do it, but I wouldn't want to do it regardless."

Renaldo and Latanya were later married and had several kids. Thanks to the support structure Renaldo and his wife built around him, he was able to have a long career in the NFL. He has since retired and had many lasting memories. However, much of that was due to the efforts of people who cared about him and wanted him to be successful. As you build your personal team, make sure that you find the right people to be on your side, especially if you choose to date and get married. Those you choose to date or be your spouse can make or break your athletic career.

# CHAPTER 19

## God

**IT WAS A SATURDAY NIGHT IN NOVEMBER**. The season had ended, but the players at Alpharetta Youth Football Association hadn't yet returned their pads. One of the opposing coaches and I had called each other, and someone suggested we do a draft and hold an all-star game. We went down our lists, held a two-team draft, and then called our players to tell them that they had been selected. We started practice on Monday.

Because it almost didn't happen, many felt it was a game that didn't really mean anything. Fortunately, the guys I drafted were workers. We went with full pads and actually worked and ran drills during practice. The other coach did mostly walk-throughs. He had some talent and he wanted to conserve their energy. We both had two different philosophies and different strategies. Either way, we were going to have a game on Saturday night to determine a winner.

When the game began, you could feel the talent on the field. I told my guys that this was a game of all-stars, but which team of all-stars was going to win? Were they going to come together to make it happen? It was all up to them. Very shortly, our team took the lead. We ran the ball well and our strategy was working. The other team's speed was bottled up because our defense played together. During the first half, a magical feeling permeated the atmosphere.

Everyone associated with that game, whether they were players, coaches, parents, referees, or park administrators, could feel that something special was happening.

When halftime rolled around, we went into the locker room in a close matchup, but we were ahead. I didn't want us to lose, and I knew that it all depended upon our willingness to play together. "Again, show me that you are the true all-stars because you can play together," I said.

Across the hall, the other coach yelled. "We're not losing this game!" he said. "If we lose this game, you're all coming out here tomorrow to run gassers!"

"Uh, Coach," one player chimed in. "The season is over after this."

"I don't care! You're all running gassers tomorrow at seven in the morning if we don't win this game!"

When the second half began, so did the hitting. For a game that almost didn't happen, all of a sudden nothing else mattered. Everybody was focused with mind, body, and spirit. The parents were engaged. Camcorders were recording. Players were intense. Coaches were shouting orders. For a moment in time, the game was everything.

Then, one of our main weapons, our talented tailback, developed a cramp and had to leave the game. Our offense went from three- to two-dimensional quickly, and the other team began to drive. Eventually, they scored a touchdown, but they missed the extra point. Later, in the fourth quarter, they scored again to tie the game. Instead of kicking, they decided to run the ball in for the win. He went after my undersized inside linebacker on an isolation play right up the middle. Our linebacker, though, played it perfectly. He stuffed the fullback with a loud *crack!* and they didn't get the winning points. The stands went crazy!

With minutes on the clock, the score was 25-25, and we had the ball. We drove, but the time was disappearing. With seconds left, we made it down to our opponent's 30-yard line. We tried a Hail Mary pass, but it fell incomplete with no time left on the clock.

Our best player came to me with wide eyes saying, "Coach, in overtime we need to attack their left outside linebacker. I can take him!"

I looked at him and said, "I'm proud of you. Because it's an all-star game, there is no overtime. We just ended in a tie. But you and your team did great. I'm proud of how you rose to the challenge." The athlete looked disappointed but understood. Victory was not achieved by anyone that night, and yet comments made by several people indicated it was the best game they had seen all year. Years later, some of those parents, players, and park personnel would comment to me how that was the best game they had been a part of in all their athletic careers. And yet, no one won. So why was it so special?

I believe that we are happiest when we use the gifts God gave us to their fullest capabilities for the sake of each other. God gave each and every one of us talents of mind, body, and spirit. When we bring each of those talents to the front of our being, especially for the sake of those we care about, I don't think anything else makes us feel more alive. And, in a game in which every person is putting all his talents into a focused event, we feel fully alive because we are fully human. Finally, as we experience the glory of the talents God gave us, we experience a part of His glory as well. It's not a religious experience, but when it all comes together, it's about as close to one as you can get.

And that's the beauty of being an athlete. You get to experience all the gifts of mind, body, and spirit within a competitive setting to find out what you can do. You'll make mistakes, and you'll have challenges. Your true character will be revealed. And, you'll find out what you're made of. What choices you make will define your future. Will you be a part of a team, or will it all be about you? Who do you give your thanks to when you win? Who do you give glory to when you lose? Did you do your best? Were you thankful for the opportunity? Did you use your mind and your spirit as well as your body? Did you help others to get better? Are you thankful for your opponent for making you better? Have you told God you're thankful for the gifts He gave you? Have you told God you're thankful for your weaknesses, so He can have glory through you as you work to improve upon them?

It can be fun to be an athlete. It can also be scary. So much can be involved, and you can't know it all. However, so much can be wonderful and can give you experiences you'll never forget. As I've written this book, I've shared many different experiences. All of them involved a relationship in some form or fashion with someone on my team.

Never forget, however, that God is also on your team. In fact, He might just surprise you as He did me one fall in 1996. We were getting ready to play the University of Washington on our home field. Practices were over for the week, and on Fridays after lunch I would walk from the dining hall, past the library and "Touchdown Jesus," towards the stadium, and to the Athletic and Convocation Center to get my football equipment. Then I would take it back across the street to the stadium locker room.

At the time, the University of Washington football team was ranked #16 in the country. We were ranked #12 after having suffered a tough defeat the week before. Being a walk-on, I knew that games against Top 20 opponents were critical. Coaches are hired or fired depending on their records, and after a loss there would be no mercy. We had to win. With me not being very high up on the depth chart, I was walking toward the stadium thinking that my week was pretty much over, and I had a free sideline pass to tomorrow's game, and that was it.

All of a sudden it hit me. I was walking away from Touchdown Jesus towards the stadium when I heard a voice from above tell me, "You are going to play tomorrow." It was very deep and clear and probably the most real sound I had ever heard. It was like a decree from above, and my entire being knew it was going to happen.

And yet, just like most of the characters in Scripture, I began to argue with it. "But they are ranked #16 in the country! I'm just a walk-on. We'd have to be leading by 28 points at halftime, and that's never going to happen." The more I argued, though, the more I listened to my heart, and I knew it was going to happen. Finally I looked up, said, "Okay, God. Whatever you say, I'll be ready for it," and walked to pick up my equipment with a secret I didn't dare share.

I moved my equipment to the stadium and walked back to my dorm room. My roommate was there, and I felt I just had to tell him something, so I said, "I think I am going to play tomorrow," to which he quickly replied, "Yeah. Right." Still in awe, I just nodded my head and went back to my responsibilities.

The next day, we had our team breakfast, went to Mass, did the walk towards the stadium between hundreds of faithful fans, and entered the stadium. Every few moments I would look at the sky and think to myself, "Are you sure, God? I mean, they are #16 in the country." There was no reply, but I wondered if He was smiling. As I suited up, I got ready as though it would come true. If I was going to play, I had to be ready.

We went through our pregame rituals and warm-ups. There was no fantastic speech for me to remember before the game because all I could think of was that voice. The sound still echoed in my being. When we ran out on the field, all I could think of was how it was going to come true. Somehow, I knew that it would.

Sure enough, when we kicked the ball off, the game immediately went our way. Very shortly, we scored four quick touchdowns and had a 28-0 lead. Midway in the second quarter, I looked at Coach Lou Holtz. He turned around and announced to his assistant coaches, "I want all the walk-ons to play!" Immediately, the assistant coaches were working on getting us all in the game. It was actually happening!

We had a blast. Guys who never saw the field covered kickoffs, punts, and played offense and defense in front of 60,000 fans and a national TV audience on NBC. We got bloodied and bruised. We competed and battled with everything we had. In the end, we won the game 54-20. It was a great experience, but for me I recognized that God smiled on us that day. Somehow, watching us play gave Him joy. I don't think He cared who won, only that He could watch us play.

And that, in the end, is what I think true happiness is: living our lives for each other and playing for the glory of God. Is there really anything else more satisfying?

# CHAPTER 20
## Go and Play

**BEING AN ATHLETE IS ONLY ONE PART** of being human, but being human is every part of being an athlete. As you learn the physics of the world and how your body physically moves, you gain an appreciation of your Creator and why you are performing your ART on the world stage. How well you appreciate your Creator gives you an appreciation for how best to move and perform with ease.

As you get involved with other people, your relationships with them determine your support structure. Sometimes you'll have to work with people who can make things difficult for you due to the way the structure works, but by being prepared and building a good support structure of solid relationships, you give yourself the best chance at not being derailed by politics or dangerous influences.

By appreciating your opponent and understanding his relationship to you, you give yourself a chance to see your own strengths and weaknesses, and you find ways to become better thanks to his willingness to compete with you.

If you understand the team relationship, you will remember that you have value even in the face of injury or lesser talent. Your body is your own. Learn how best to develop it for what it is, not according to a standard that isn't yours. Have a good relationship with yourself.

Have a relationship with God. Playing sports is a gift that allows us to experience mind, body, and spirit all at the same time. We discover things about ourselves that we didn't know, and we find that playing for each other is the best feeling we can have even if nobody wins the game.

And finally, remember that somewhere up above is a loving God who made you and loves nothing more than watching you play. Now, go and Play with Confidence!

# ACKNOWLEDGMENTS

There are so many individuals to thank for the completion of this project. First and foremost, thank you God. Remember that night when I was seventeen and I drove to the middle of the desert furious at you for not making me six-foot five like my father? My road would be far tougher because people would always say I wouldn't be big enough. Yet, through all that, you stuck with me and showed me what I needed to know. Had the road been easier, I probably wouldn't have appreciated all my experiences and this book would never have happened.

Secondly, RaDonna, my wife, thank you. I know you suffered with me through the years as I've been torn between sports and the real world. You, though, have always been an inspiration to me, and I wanted to be my best self for you. Somehow, someway, this book is a culmination of that, and I couldn't have done it without you. You're my love, and I'm honored to be your husband and to have you as my wife.

Thank you, Van Kottis. I had been writing this over the course of several years, yet you gave me the courage to finish the project. Sometimes we're afraid of the talents God put inside us, and yet we need others to help reignite the spark. You helped light that spark, and I thank you.

To Ron Wallace, thank you. I wanted to get a perspective from someone outside the sports world, and you helped me understand that this book isn't just for sports, but for life. Your thoughts and courage helped me to push through even though it was difficult.

Thank you, Carolyn Aspensen. Going through the publishing process isn't easy, and you took time out of your busy schedule to offer advice as to how to proceed. I know you'll do great things as an author, and I thank you for helping with this project.

To Coach Lou Holtz and Coach Ara Parseghian, thank you. From my father and me, it was an honor to play for you at Notre Dame. Many of the lessons we learned from you influenced us to do our best, and you were there for us at very influential times in our lives. I'm so honored to have both of you as a part of this project. My hope is that the lessons you taught us will be available for others through the ages. Thank you.

Thank you, Booktrope, for taking me on as an author. Thank you, Katie Wacek. I know you're as excited as I am about this project and I still believe you'll finish that marathon one day. Thank you, Christina Correnti. Your work helped make this project much better than I could have done on my own. Thank you, Bob Meyers, for letting me include your photo for the "about the author" section. And thank you Greg Simanson. Your cover rocks!

For everyone who chose to endorse this book, thank you! I'm so very honored to have you be a part of this project, and I know you're doing it because you care about people. Thank you!

For all my teammates and coaches at the youth levels, Bishop Gorman High School, the University of Notre Dame, and in the adult recreation leagues. Thank you. Whether we won or lost, got along or didn't, we did it together. Every moment is a memory I will keep with me, and I still regard you as my teammates and coaches even though we no longer wear the same uniform.

To all the guys I coached with at the Alpharetta Youth Football Association and at Chattahoochee High School. Thank you. Though we all were in the business of making judgments, I want you to know that I was always the hardest judge on myself. I learned something from all of our successes and our mistakes, and whether we won or lost, I wouldn't want to do it with a different group of guys. I'd be honored to coach with each of you again. Just know that now since I wrote a book, I'll be coming at it using these principles.

Thank you to all my Kunz Football clients and business partners. I never imagined I'd at one time have a business doing private sports instruction, but your faith in me helped me to perfect the lessons in this book over three years. You showed me that even someone who doesn't have great athletic ability can excel, so long as they have the right attitude and someone in their corner that cares enough to show them the proper way. All of you are an inspiration.

Thank you to all my competition throughout the years, either as a player or a coach. Whether I liked you or not, I always respected your abilities. Know that I prepared hard for everything you might do because I knew that you had the ability to be great. I always expected your best, and that helped me to try to be my best. Thank you.

Thank you to all my players throughout the years. I learned something from each of you. In fact, every one of you has greatness inside of you. You have only to believe it's there and to have the courage to bring it out!

Finally, thank you Mom and Dad. I've dedicated this book to you because I never could have learned to look for the principles inside this book unless you first took the time to show me how. Learning first begins with observation, and I learned first and foremost from watching the character inside both of you. Thank you.

# ABOUT THE AUTHOR

Business man, City Councilman, volunteer, coach, and former football player, Matt Kunz understands what it takes to win on and off the field. He was a letter winner as a walk-on football player and played linebacker and special teams for the Fighting Irish of Notre Dame, where he holds a Bachelor of Arts degree in American Studies.

Through sports, Matt, the son of former Atlanta Falcon and Baltimore Colt George Kunz and Gainesville native Mary Sue, learned valuable lessons about leadership, politics, and coaching. For several years, he was an active football coach. He worked with players aged six to twenty-six, ranging in experience from youth, high school, college, and semi-professional. He also offered private football lessons to athletes in the area through a part-time business he founded in 2006.

Matt, his wife RaDonna, and their family dogs, live in Milton, Georgia. A frequent speaker, Matt motivates and encourages individuals to be the best they can be on and off the field.

Follow Matt on Twitter at @MattKunz59.

# MORE PRAISE FOR *TRIUMPH!*

"What an inspirational book! *Triumph!* truly reminds us what it means to be alive in mind, body, and spirit!

—**Father Jason Brooks**, Priest and former college football player

"I love the game of football. However, when I was in high school I was not as tall or big as the other players on the team. My family met Coach Kunz, who had been watching me practice and saw potential in me. Since I was undersized and did not have the power or speed of other players, Coach shared and demonstrated his knowledge of football with me. This was important because it kept me mentally one step ahead of my opponent. Coach Kunz guided me through training and focused on the fundamentals of the game. His one-on-one training made me a better and more informed player. With this knowledge I became Defensive Player of the Year in my junior year of high school, and in my senior year I had the second most tackles on the team.

"Matt Kunz has a passion for the game of football, and he shares his knowledge with young players. Not only has Coach Kunz been a great trainer, but he has also been a mentor for me and many other young student athletes."

—**Ryan Gehricke**, junior, University of Alabama, criminal justice major

"Having coached football with Matt, I've had the pleasure of witnessing first-hand how his straightforward coaching philosophy has inspired passion, leadership, courage, and humility in his players. This same coaching philosophy can be found in *Triumph!*, a book designed for the athlete to help conquer the greatest obstacles and achieve the ultimate goals."

—**Ed Nejeschleba**, former youth football and basketball coach

"I've known Matt and his father for many years, and I can tell you that the advice in *Triumph!* is sound. Anyone who reads this book will have the potential to do great things in their sport. More importantly, they will be better people for having read it."

—**Mark Smith**, business owner & Chairman of the Scott C. Ratterman/C. Edward Shell Memorial Scholarship Fund, 35-year football official, 2x State Champion

"Matt's book is a MUST READ for any devoted football fan or player and especially for parents of football players. It explains the ART of football in a new and entertaining way, but in addition, it is a primer for how to be a successful athlete, as well as a successful person."

—**Judy Kelner**, football fanatic, parent and grandparent of football players, from Pop Warner through college

"As a parent of two daughters, one a state champion high school tennis player and the other a southeast region dance champion, I only wish that we'd had Matt's book before our girls embarked upon their journeys. Our family has dealt with many coaches, from bad to outstanding, and the choices one makes in selecting a coach, an instructor, a team, etc. Matt's book boils it all down in a common sense way. Unfortunately, there's politics in everything, and sports are no exception. Matt's book should be read by all athletes over the age of 12 and their parents."

—**Michael Rosenthal**, attorney at Wagner, Johnston & Rosenthal, P.C.

"Books like *Triumph!* don't come around all too often, but I'm so glad this one did! *Triumph!* answered all of my questions about the inner workings of sports. This is a must read for the athlete who wants to bring out the most of their God-given talent, the parent who wants to understand how best to direct their child in the game they love, and the coach who wants to triumph on and off the field."

—**Van J. Kottis**, former sports player, current softball coach, sports fan, and parent

"To all who read this book, you have given yourself a tremendous advantage in sports—and in life. My dear friend Matt Kunz has made plain for you wisdom I wish I had as an athlete both in high school and in college at the University of Notre Dame. Kunz combines personal success and experiences as a player and coach, wisdom from professional athletes and famous coaches, inspiring stories, and practical strategies into a solid guide for navigating through life as an athlete. The question is, will you heed his advice? Don't be the athlete wondering what could have been. Use your God-given ability to learn how to prepare advantageously for athletic competition and for life as an athlete. Regardless of whether you become a professional, you are an athlete, and the world will treat you differently. Learn how to be successful on and off the field by reading this book. If you were guaranteed victory, would you read it? Your odds of victory increase greatly if you know what to expect. I'm honored to be teammates with Kunz to this day, and I so value his wisdom. His trust in and obedience to God, as well as his leadership and courage to speak up enabled me to become a starter at Notre Dame, and I know his advice will help you succeed as well. Thank you, God, and thank you, Matt Kunz! Forever, I am grateful."

—**Bryan Mulvena**, MBA, Notre Dame BSME '00, Notre Dame Football '96–'97

# MORE GREAT READS
# FROM BOOKTROPE

*Heart and Sole: How 26 Ran Their First Marathon (And You Can, Too)* **by Melinda Hinson Neely** (Non-Fiction) Heart and Sole is THE source of inspiration and practical information for anyone aspiring to run a marathon, a 26.2 mile journey that will change your life.

*Home Field – Writers Remember Baseball* **by John Douglas Marshall** (Memoir - Sports) Nine great writers, including two National Book Award winners, reminisce about their own experiences with America's national pastime.

*The First Father Abraham* **by Henry Hanoch Abramovitch** (Nonfiction - Religious Studies) An interdisciplinary retelling of Abraham's adulthood that provides a new perspective on Abraham, founder of religious traditions, and a study of family dynamics, faith, and leadership.

*The Heart of Power* **by John Thomas Wood** (Personal Growth) Discover the basis for your power, the form it takes and the results of power, both in yourself and those around you.

*The Heart of Fear* **by John Thomas Wood** (Personal Growth) Fear is an emotion we should not deny, but we shouldn't let it run our lives.

Discover more books and learn about our
new approach to publishing at **www.booktrope.com.**

Made in the USA
Charleston, SC
28 September 2015